Trolls
and
Truth

Trolls
and
Truth

14 Realities about today's church that we don't want to see

Jimmy Dorrell

NEW HOPE
PUBLISHERS

Birmingham, Alabama

New Hope® Publishers
P. O. Box 12065
Birmingham, AL 35202-2065
www.newhopepublishers.com

Library of Congress Cataloging-in-Publication Data

Dorrell, Jimmy, 1950-
  Trolls and truth : 14 realities about today's church that we don't
want to see / Jimmy Dorrell.
       p. cm.
  Includes bibliographical references.
  ISBN-13: 978-1-59669-010-3 (softcover)
  ISBN-10: 1-59669-010-0 (soft cover)
  1. Non-church-affiliated people--Texas--Waco. 2. Evangelistic
work--Texas--Waco. 3. Preaching to non-church-affiliated people. I.
Title.
BV4921.3.D67 2006
277.64'2840829--dc22
                          2006014361

ISBN-10: 1-59669-010-0
ISBN-13: 978-1-59669-010-3
N064142•0906•6M1

Dedication

Dedicated to my friends, mentors, and brothers and
sisters at Church Under the Bridge, Waco, Texas,
who have taught me about the kingdom of God.

table of contents

foreword

Rarely do we find a man who is both a strategist and a practitioner. Each of these qualities are often found dominant in one person, but seldom are both found in equal measure! When we planted a "new wineskin" cell church community in Houston, Jimmy and Janet Dorrell were brought into the team to form cell groups among high school students. Their equipping ministry grew so rapidly that within a year and a half they had more than 600 students in cells. He even made the front page of the newspaper and was voted to speak at commencement services, an honor usually reserved for a pastor of a huge church or a politician.

Jimmy and Janet left us to return to Waco, Texas, driven by their mandate to bring renewal not only to the forgotten poor but also to the dismal slums of the community. With great sacrifice, they have stayed by their divinely assigned task for many years. They formed a community with other couples who moved into the neglected area. They trained sophisticated college students to understand poverty by putting them on the streets for a couple of days with empty pockets. When the homeless sleeping under a bridge came to their attention, they formed the Church Under the Bridge, a cavern that became a sanctuary under Interstate 35. For their tenth anniversary, I was the guest speaker for this body of Christ; to my amazement I met not only bikers, alcoholics, old women with shopping carts holding their possessions, but also a county judge! Jackie Pullinger, who ministers to addicts in Hong Kong, has written, "If you want to attract the rich, serve the poor."

A house for recovering addicts, renovating of shacks into livable quarters, job-training classes, and other projects that give hope to the poor were methodically put into place by this amazing couple. At the same time, Jimmy earned a doctorate at the local seminary and joined the faculty to train potential pastors.

Their burden to reach the poor has carried Jimmy and Janet to minister in far corners of the earth, including India. I shall never forget boarding a flight in Singapore and finding Janet there, en route to Waco from north India! They take teams of students to foreign countries to be exposed to poverty. They serve international foods to those who are trained in Waco, where some must eat strange food with their fingers instead of forks.

Jimmy's ability to be both a strategist and a practitioner has been recognized, leading to significant grants from foundations to further expand the ministries in Waco. The ministry has gained multiple buildings through the years, including a large Presbyterian church that has been renovated to be a center for reducing the poverty percentage of the population.

When Jimmy and Janet came to work on our Houston team back in the 1970s, Janet was a strikingly beautiful young woman. As the years have passed, Jimmy's beard has turned white and Janet now shows a few wrinkles formed by years of being among the poor, living simply so others might simply live. Her beauty is enhanced by each line on her face, formed while she has loved the unlovely.

In this book, you will learn what the poor have taught Jimmy and Janet about the church and the urgency to learn biblical truths and fresh ways of being God's people on earth. *Trolls and Truth* points the way to radical transformation of church life. The author hasn't just preached it—he has lived it.

Dr. Ralph W. Neighbour
Houston, Texas, 2006

acknowledgements

This book is written from the joys and struggles of a lifetime of believing that the church is God's primary sign of His kingdom on the earth. One cannot read the Book of Acts about the early church and realize how far we have strayed from that organic expression of being the viable and visible witness of the body of Christ. Through centuries of institutionalism and cultural compromise, what began as a natural expression of a supernatural community seems to have been lost, found, and lost again, over and over.

So the church exists today, particularly in the Western culture, on shifting sand and shallow precepts. With the postmodern era growing in influence, many suggest that the church as we know it has lost its voice and will likely never have center stage again. Though perhaps the church as we know it will never again speak from a base of power and cultural authority, it cannot and will not cease to exist or completely lose its radical message, because it is still the Bride of Christ. It is connected to the source of Truth that withstands all complicity and compromise. The Spirit of Truth will continue to remind, encourage, challenge, and disrupt the patterns of the church that belie its eternal message. And that same Spirit will often use unexpected sources to make the point that the church inevitably has a different value system, one which is counter-cultural and profound.

These stories of rebels and misfits who have refused to accept the church as it is, and have given their lives on behalf of what could be, have inspired and encouraged me. From the apostle Paul, who admonished Peter when he retreated to the comfort of his Jewish friends, to the friends in our own lives who remind us that words can be cheap when there is little action, these are the ones who have shaped me. I acknowledge the hundreds of men and women throughout church history who stood up for the truth, even when it cost them dearly. I recognize Martin Luther, John Calvin, Nikolaus von Zinzendorf, the Anabaptists of the Radical Reformation, John Wesley, and hundreds of other radicals who refused to accept "what is" as the truth. I am especially thankful for those pioneers and authors of "new wineskins" in the late 1960s and early 1970s who wrote books about the renewal of the church that gave me hope, when my direction was toward cynicism.

I particularly want to acknowledge the voiceless poor of our world who live and die without fanfare. It is often in those slums, barrios, and housing projects of our world where the truth of the kingdom shines forth. No one knows these people's names except the King, but these followers have embraced His ways, His values, and His truth, even in the midst of hunger, sickness and seeming hopelessness. These people will sit at the banquet table.

The stories in this book are true-life accounts of friends who have taught me what no seminary could. In their profound simplicity, I have learned about God and His ways. From the poor, ex-offender, mentally ill, and drug addict, I have learned how to forgive, laugh, cry, and worship. I have seen God in them.

This journey has been a family pilgrimage. Beginning with our move into the inner city over 28 years ago, my wife and children have been walking alongside me in this journey. Our children, Seth, Josh, Zach, and Christy, have grown up in a diverse and economically challenged neighborhood, yet have acknowledged it as their own neighborhood without resentment. They have fed strangers at the front door, greeted prostitutes on the street, and played basketball with young people our society has rejected. They have put up with my sermons under a bridge, the only church they know as children.

No better life partner could ever be found to travel this unique and challenging path than my wife and joy of my life, Janet. She has lived out what I often feel I preach but rarely do. She has gone out to the streets early in the morning to encourage the prostitute. She has written, sung, and played on her guitar songs of the kingdom for these 28 years of marriage. She has walked the buffalo paths of the unreached people group in India that our little church has adopted, put bandages on the villager in Haiti, and hugged a hundred orphans each year in Mexico City. Most of all, she has passionately shared life with me and lived out the truths of this book.

introduction

MY mother often read fairy tales to my brothers and me each night on my parents' big bed. The lucid images of giants, fairies, leprechauns, mermaids, pirates, ghosts, and witches filled our childhood imaginations as we vicariously entered the stories. But the great, ugly troll in the old, Norwegian story of "The Three Billy Goats Gruff" always scared me more than all the other storybook creatures. Who was this horrible creature, "with eyes as big as saucers and a nose as long as a poker," that lived under a bridge and threatened to gobble up the innocent, hungry goats seeking to become fat on the grassy hillside across the bridge? Who would even live under a common bridge at all and then threaten the playful, innocent animal kingdom with such taunts? So, I was delighted when the biggest of the three billy goats accepted the challenge of the ugly troll and crushed his body "and poked his eyes out with his horns." We were all "happy ever after."

In 1978, out of conviction that our call was among the poor, my wife and I moved into an impoverished neighborhood in Waco, Texas, where we have lived ever since. Frustrated with church work, which sometimes seemed to inhibit the very thing I felt called to do, I took a job by day as a program developer and grant writer for a social services agency. But our ministry was among the poor neighbors where we shared life. After eight years, God provided a way to live out our vocation full time through the creation and funding of Mission Waco, an interdenominational urban ministry to the poor and marginalized. We began to try to see who the unchurched poor were in our community.

Within six months, we discovered a small group of homeless men who had fallen asleep half-intoxicated under an interstate bridge. On September 20, 1992, these five troll-like, homeless men met my wife and me for a Bible study under a noisy, graveled underpass. I have no recollection of what was taught or discussed, but something happened that day that forever changed all of us. Each Sunday morning afterwards, a few more homeless and disenfranchised folks wandered under the bridge to see what was happening and engage in the dialogue. A few weeks later, a couple from the community joined us. Soon a couple of university students sat down in the growing circle of metal chairs. Through the weeks and months, this ragtag group of misfits grew in numbers. A car battery to power a cheap microphone was purchased to overcome the noise of the zoom of 18-wheelers overhead. Three Baylor University law students brought sandwiches for the growing number of poor who came. As we became a community of care, reports of those who were missing due to incarceration, crisis, or moving on were shared and remembered in prayer. Something genuine and powerful was happening here. And the circle grew.

What started as a tiny Bible study became Church Under the Bridge (CUB) within a year or two. Now a church of over 300 folks, the congregation meets 52 weeks a year outside under the same Interstate 35 bridge. Rain or shine, hot or cold, the concrete sanctuary is open for all to worship.

Each Sunday morning there are cars jumping the curb to park, trailers of chairs and portable toilets pulled to the fringes, and a flatbed trailer set with microphones, speakers, drums, and scaffolding. At the opposite end, three tables are arranged with hot food to serve at least 100 of those who came for their first and perhaps only meal for the day. On the side is a "recovery Bible study" for some 30 folks who struggle with addiction. Across the way a nurse is cleaning and covering an infected, open wound of one of the men who was jumped the night before.

Like ants, everyone seems to be moving around. Children are running, adults are laughing and visiting, and chairs are being positioned around the massive cement pillars to accommodate the congregation. Feedback from the speakers shriek and congregants know that it is almost time to begin the worship service. A guitar strum, a drumbeat, a violin chord . . . ready!

For the next 90 minutes, this ordinary bridge is made holy by the presence of the Spirit of God inhabiting the praises of these insignificant people; lively singing, testimonies of change, a poorly scripted skit, prayers of repentance, a challenging sermon on following Jesus, the bread and juice of communion, and hugs all around.

Church Under the Bridge is a church. According to an article in the April 2004 issue of *Christianity Today*, "CUB's calling is to be a church to the unchurched of all socioeconomic levels and races and to serve the poor and marginalized. Ex-prisoners and food stamp recipients worship with the well-heeled and educated." Without steeple or "church clothes," something genuinely New Testament happens each week in this open-air tabernacle with 18-wheelers zooming overhead and a ragtag congregation below. In this concrete wasteland, "God is doing a new thing" (Isaiah 43:19) among the marginalized and mainstream, "black, white, and brown; rich and poor; educated in the streets and the university." This unusual model of church renewal has emerged as yet another evidence of God's dynamic and organic body of "called-out ones." Purpose driven they are, yet not from a book study or accountability group, but from an intuitive rightness that somehow guides culturally and economically diverse followers of Jesus to know it is good to be together as brothers and sisters despite the differences.

The people of Church Under the Bridge are comfortable joking about being like trolls, having church under a bridge. The best gifts of those who attend are their humility and recognition that God often does use the least and the unusual to show His ways. Being a "troll" is an acknowledgement of Paul's profound words, "Up to this moment we have become the scum of the earth, the refuse of this world" (1 Corinthians 4:13). Being a fool for Christ is a badge of honor, not humiliation. Trolls never think of themselves as big shots who deserve something. Their sense of unworthiness is the very character trait that makes them worthy.

Truth in Different Clothing

This book is, in a sense, written by these trolls. Ironically, these modern trolls have become the teachers of truth to us "billy goats," trampling through life to get fat on the hillside. Lessons are being learned about kingdom values and how to really be the people of God. Lessons are being taught by the "least of these" to those of us who thought we knew something. Paul was right when he said, "Those parts of the body that seem to be weaker are indispensable" (1 Corinthians 12:22).

Their communication is often crude and straightforward, with few innuendos and courtesies. They just speak truth bluntly. If I preach a bad sermon one Sunday, they tell me. If the church proclaims something they think is hypocritical, we hear it. Packaged in colorful

language and searing insight, the poor and disenfranchised say what they think and let us
worry about sorting through the details. But
what they say is worthy of hearing, for these are
the discerning folks who see things through raw
simplicity. Wordsmiths cannot get past them.

This book is also *about* these indispensable trolls; those often maligned and rejected
creatures of our world represented by the not-
so-pretty or not-so-socially-appropriate people
of our society who offer us truth in different
clothing. And while the Norwegian legend
lifts the billy goat as the hero, the kingdom of
God gives new lens to the storybook tale and
proclaims value to the widow, the leper, the
prisoner, and the prostitute. The marginalized
troll-like folks in the upside-down order of God
remind those of us who think we know something that the pearls of great price are often
hidden from the arrogant and proud. "Listen,
my dear brothers: Has not God chosen those
who are poor in the eyes of the world to be rich
in faith and to inherit the kingdom he promised those who love him?" (James 2:5).

In this book, you will enter the lives of
troll-like men and women who have struggled
in the world, yet come to understand some of
the profound truths of the kingdom of God and

His church. In each chapter, I tell the story of one person I met through CUB and the truth that God chose to share with me through that person. You may be offended by the bluntness of their insights. Or you may be convicted that they are right, but feel trapped by a lifetime of complicity with compromises. But either way, you will be urged toward a refreshing honesty and challenged to ask the hard questions again about what really matters.

The tension between the traps of institutional Christendom and vital church are real and cannot be ignored. Though I am not suggesting we burn or sell our buildings and fire our hired clergy, most of us churched folks must admit that intuitively we know that what we have become is far less that we are called to be. To not listen or acknowledge the half-truths we have adopted makes us less than the "called-out ones." The unpretentious folks featured in these pages have less to lose and can say their truths more profoundly. The question is, have our ears become too deaf to hear?

The western church is in trouble

For most of Christendom's 2,000 years, biblical insights have come from the literate, the verbal and the influential. Councils have debated doctrinal tensions of the faith, pastors, prophets, and evangelists have proclaimed vital or ignored profundities, and authors have captured historical truths and biblical ideas with pen on page. Indeed, we are indebted to these who have sacrificially worked to transmit this upside down kingdom of God.

Ironically, however, Jesus used the misfits of His society to teach the profound truths of the Father, lessons which were hard for the religious to comprehend. A demoniac, a leper, a prostitute, a beggar, a poor widow, a tax collector, a fisherman, and an old woman bleeding to death in the streets—these were His conveyors of radical truth. And they still are.

The church in America is in trouble. There are many reasons, but perhaps none so flagrant as the disregard of these unrecognized teachers from our midst. Isolated in gated communities and gentrified neighborhoods, most affluent Christians have been anesthetized by pretty words and pretty people and follow a distorted gospel. Yet it seems to be the misfits, the broken, and the marginalized that cause us to look and really see, listen and really hear, and really reevaluate who we are in the prism of this inclusive gospel. Those without degrees or etiquette or business cards become our best mentors.

Particularly for the evangelical church, the great reversal, prompted by the social gospel movement of the early 1900s had an enormous effect on the church and how it saw its mission in the world. In fear of being labeled a liberal, the conservative church tragically turned away from most involvement with social concerns. Emphasis shifted to a greater emphasis on evangelism and personal faith. The lack of significant impact on the world was due to a myopic theology that focused on heaven and neglected "thy kingdom come on earth as it is in heaven." According to Ray Bakke in *A Theology as Big as the City*,

> After surveys in some fifty cities it was clear that 85–90% of all major barriers to effective urban ministry are not in the cities at all—they are inside our churches. The schism in the church that has pitted social and personal ministries against each other in the city is a tragic legacy of the fundamentalist-modernist controversy early in the twentieth century, still marginalizes the church's ministry in the rapidly urbanizing developing world. The church must learn how to go up

to the urban powerful and down to the urban powerless with equal integrity.

According to the book *Missional Church,* edited by Darrell L. Guder, "Understanding the church as an alternative culture for the sake of missional faithfulness goes against the grain of the dominant Western culture and its legacy of Christendom."

Transformation in the church must come. "It is hard to escape the conclusion that one of the greatest roadblocks to the gospel of Jesus Christ is the institutional church," says Howard Snyder in *Radical Renewal.* In new wineskins and perhaps through the life of an old wino, our ecclesiology must be upended by the "least of these": the hungry, imprisoned, sick, and stranger. Intentional efforts in local congregations must be made to reconnect the rich and the poor; the black, white, and brown; those educated in the university; and those educated on the streets. Only then can we learn the lessons that this God of the little people wants us to know.

How Did we Get Here?

Grounded in a Hebraic theology of holism, which refuses to separate body, mind, and soul in the individual, word and deed were biblically integrated. Yet the very sinful nature of humans naturally tends to divide cognitive awareness and obedient action. Information and action are uniquely one. Biblically, to know God was to do the will of God. According to the book *Planting and Growing Urban Churches,* edited by Harvie Conn, "Hebraic thinking focuses on fusion rather than fission, synthesis rather than analysis, institution rather empiricism, system rather than segment."

Adam and Eve's sin, Cain's assault, Abraham's lie, Noah's drunkenness, and Moses' impatience all remind us of our failure to integrate life into this seamless whole. The eighth-century prophets had condemned similar behavior. Israel's self-righteousness as God's chosen people had hardened their ethical behavior to the point where the haves felt no responsibility for the have-nots. Though clearly the Deuteronomic and Levitical law had outlined how the poor were to be treated and served, religious gluttony had lulled the pious to ignore the needs of the poor and disenfranchised. Injustice prevailed in their business practices, legal wranglings, and moral behavior to the point when God terminated His contract with Israel and promised their demise. They just could not seem to remember that believing and doing go hand in hand.

Though Bible scholars tend to disagree how much the shift of Christianity from the Hebrew worldview to the Greek worldview affected its distortion, most all agree that Western Christians have never understood the seamless integration of faith and practice that was basic to the Bible times. As most of the persecuted Christians escaped from Jerusalem, they encountered the Hellenistic mind-sets of Greece and Rome. "The theology of Augustine could not but spawn a dualistic view of reality, which became second nature in Western Christianity—the tendency to regard salvation as a private matter," says David J. Bosch in *Transforming Mission*. Already struggling in A.D. 70 with doing instead of listening and talking, James reminds the church that religion was not "Gnostic" (knowing), but doing the truth. Being religious to James meant nothing less than the practical work of taking care of widows and orphans, watching your language, and avoiding cultural compromise (James 1:26, 27). John echoed the same sentiments, reminding the early Christians that having material possessions required sharing those resources with those who had need. "Dear children, let us not love with words or tongue, but with actions and in truth" (1 John 3:18). To ignore the physical

Introduction

needs of the poor was to deny faith in God! His words became even stronger during his exile on Patmos. "Because you are lukewarm—neither hot nor cold—I am about to spit you out of my mouth. You say, 'I am rich; I have acquired wealth and do not need a thing.' But you do not realize that you are wretched, pitiful, poor, blind and naked" (Revelation 3:17).

A holistic, biblical theology will bring us back to a healthy integration of word and deed. "Holistic ministry, empowered by the power of the Spirit, is about creating samples and signs of God's new day in everyday settings. It is about the restoration of life in its fullness," according to the book *The Urban Face of Mission*, edited by Harvie Conn.

syncretism

Every worldview struggles with the insidiousness of syncretism, which blends beliefs and cultural values together. One's provincial preferences tend to distort or change the foundational truths of personal religious doctrine, which inhibit the preferred lifestyle of the follower. Rarely does one diametrically oppose a religious truth, but more often tends to dilute its content with compromise or special circumstances. Like a cultural virus, the closely held values of each society tend to infect the purity of the dominant religion's dogma. More than contextualization, which helps a society understand a truth in its own culture, syncretism distorts the essence of that sacred truth by reshaping it around cultural norms.

For example, where Christianity has been adopted in animistic cultures, syncretism tends to promote spiritism, with charms, curses, tradition, and magic continuing as practices of the believer. A cultural anthropologist who examines the Catholic Church in Haiti finds the practice of voodoo normative among churchgoers, who make secret visits to the witch doctor for remedies or healing. In France, the same evaluator would find that, though married and buried in the church building, most so-called Christians rarely attend church or believe in a sovereign, personal God. They are postmodern and "post-Christian" in their worldview and may even be considered practical atheists by most theologians. Little of the Christian worldview actually shapes their daily practices.

In the materialistic Western world, individualism, progress, logic, and privatization of faith became the prevalent by-products of the Enlightenment. Modernity reshaped the uncompromising values of the early church, described in the Book of Acts, to become more user-friendly for our consumer-oriented culture unaccustomed to sacrifice and suffering. Success, defined by cultural standards, drove our choices, even in religious matters. While belief in God became, and still is, an expected norm for the masses of America, actually following the lifestyle and principles of Jesus were unusual in a culture where the gross national product and the Dow determined the day. Everyone needs God because God can help get you where you want to go. By reducing salvation to a walk down the church aisle, a verbal assent that God exists and forgives, even a water baptism, one is supposedly guaranteed the sinner's ticket to heaven. The self-proclaimed Christian could now embrace the hedonistic and self-centered values of the American life without guilt or worry of eternal consequences. With the loss of Christian community as a check and balance of biblical faith, modern churchgoers were free to decide what was best for them and their families, even when the value was virtually anti-Christian. This post-Constantinian adaptation of the teachings of Jesus developed to no less than the early church heresy of antinomianism, the belief that practice of faith was optional as long as verbal assent had been proclaimed. If the so-called Christians tried hard enough, looked good, went to church, belonged to the right groups, and saluted the American flag, who could question their faith?

The bottom line is that even though there is no cultureless gospel, the gospel cannot be determined by cultural values and remain "good news." For Christians, God is the standard that shapes the principles, the author and finisher of our faith, not the blesser of all we do. If the culture gives value to what God does not, the cultural value is a lie. If the culture ignores the ethics of the revealed truth, it can only lead to half-truths and distortion at best.

But much more than mental assent to the biblical truth, the practice of living out the ethics of the truth becomes its validation. Praxis and faith are intrinsically one. The Bible has no place for affirmation without action. To know God, biblically speaking, was to do His will. Mere cognitive assent is not faith.

upside-Down kingdom

It is at this juncture that the often-rejected ones become our mentors, for they recognize words are cheap and the church has adorned itself with costume jewelry instead of the pearl of great price. They are the "crap detectors" of life who can spot a phony a mile away. And in many cases, they have rejected the church today because of its insincerity and duplicity. Like it or not, they often say what they think and they are frequently more correct than we wish.

Those of us casually traipsing to greener and higher grass on the other side of our own bridges often forget that the kingdom of God, Jesus's primary theme, is more than a plan of salvation. It is a way of life, far different from the human tendencies, which bless power, beauty, and wealth. It is through washing feet, turning cheeks, and being last that God's order is lived. It is through humility, suffering, and brokenness that spiritual truths are found.

Thus the poor, the not-so-pretty, the ex-con, the mentally ill, and other "trolls" in our culture become our mentors, if we will listen and really hear. In these pages, there are stories of such men and women who gather under a bridge, more often feared and misunderstood by those who travel overhead than appreciated for who they are and what God does through them. But it is through them that the eschatological truths of this upside-down kingdom are found.

KRUGER'S TRUTH

LOOKS DON'T MATTER

The church has been seduced by pagan concerns of appearance and people's approval. Most of the rejected poor accept others despite their external appearance.

 I

"EXCUSE ME, SIR, are you having Bible study?" the tall, bearded man inquired. "Can I join you?" And with that, one of our best teachers sat down among us.

Kruger's life had been hard. Reared in a small Texas town, his alcoholic dad relentlessly rejected him with rarely a word of approval. Forced to go to church as a young boy, he resented every song and sermon as hypocrisy. Outward signs of religion were everywhere in this small community. Believing in Jesus was as normative as Friday night football. But with each verbal and physical beating, Kruger waited for an opportunity to leave his two-faced family. At 15 he was gone. With a few odd jobs here and there, the army became the first stable environment for him. But this stability came wrapped in the Vietnam War, alcohol, and drugs. Before a year had passed, Kruger was diagnosed with post-traumatic stress disorder (PTSD) and released back to the care of the Veterans Administration (VA).

"Certified crazy by the VA," as he said of himself, few opportunities existed to work and keep his small government allowance. Certainly there was not enough income to maintain his growing drug habit. So to the underworld he went, and Kruger became an accomplished car thief. Claiming membership in a large gang of thieves from all over the Southwest, he could steal and sell automobiles with the best of them, with plenty of cash to support his habit.

Then the inevitable happened. He was caught in Alabama in a burglary gone bad, and whisked off to jail. Using a false identity in hopes of remaining anonymous, Kruger laid down in his lonely cell. Noticing a book on the window ledge, he reached for it and thumbed through the pages. It was a Bible. "Not one in that foreign KJV language," he quipped, "but one I could read and understand." For the next three days with only short naps between chapters, he read.

Overwhelmed by the truth, he cried out to God to change him and unweave the messes of his life. "God, if You can open the door of Peter's cell, open mine." To his amazement, when he pulled on his cell door, it was unlatched. With no guards around, he walked to the end of the hall and made a collect call to his mother, requesting her to send bail money. She did and he was again free on the streets.

But something had happened in that jail cell that forever changed him. The God he thought was more like his abusing father had become a God of grace and mercy. The words of a gospel that had felt more like bad news than good news had given him a new perspective for living. He was freed on the inside as much as the outside. New life, new direction.

Traveling back to Waco, Kruger did what new Christians are supposed to do—go to church. On Sunday morning, dressed in the only clothes he owned and with his mangled beard and unwashed hair, he entered the vestibule of the first church he found. "Hey, you, mister," the assigned greeter barked, "What are you doing here?" "I just came to church," Kruger said. "Not looking like that," pointing to the clothes. "You'll have to find some church clothes and clean up if you want to come back here."

And with that, memories of his childhood flashed before him. Rejected for his soiled appearance by those who deemed themselves keepers of the earthly kingdom, this new child of God asked what many are asking today, "If I in my poverty am acceptable to God, why am I not acceptable to His people?"

In his simplicity, Kruger's question defines the challenge. Though few of us would openly acknowledge that appearance matters to God, our actions suggest otherwise. The preoccupation in Western culture with the appearance of one's outfit, house, yard, car, and office complex has affected how Christians determine their own values. What might seem like a shallow or legalistic issue unveils a basic core value that followers of the kingdom must face.

> If I in my poverty am acceptable to god, why am I not acceptable to His people?

Appearance Really Doesn't Matter (or Does It?)

From the time most babies leave the hospital, outward appearance becomes paramount. Young parents and new grandparents spend millions of dollars for infant and baby clothing that are usually loathed by the child and worn only a time or two. Yet the oohs and ahs from well-wishers of the new family are validations of this "prettiest baby I have ever seen" conditioned response. Neatly tied bows, knotted hairstyles, and well-starched outfits are hardly appreciated by the baby just leaving the comfort of the mother's womb. But from that time on, appropriate public appearance is a value embedded in life.

Americans spend millions a year on clothing that has little to do with need. Add the cost of accessorizing the outfits with belts, ties, scarves, hats, earrings, jewelry, and purses, and millions more are added. Shoe sales alone add millions more. Include the cost of haircuts, cosmetics, tanning, manicures, pedicures, and hair removal and the amount skyrockets. Name-brand and designer labels drive the fashion industry.

Even in the simple dress of Jesus's day, when clothing choices amounted to little more than a pick of robes or sashes, the issue was important enough to the Teacher that He reminded the hillside listeners of their little faith with the question, "Why do you worry about clothes? . . . Pagans run after all these things" (Matthew 6:28, 32). Concern for clothing, food, or drink is a futile endeavor, and is compared to idolatry and paganism.

Jesus chastised the religious Pharisees because of their preoccupation with outward attraction. "Woe to you, teachers of the law and Pharisees, you hypocrites! You are like whitewashed tombs, which look beautiful on the outside but on the inside are full of dead men's bones and everything unclean" (Matthew 23:2). Driven by some insatiable desire to be approved by others for what they wore instead of who they were, the issue was significant enough to the Son of God that He frequently used the concern for outward appearance as a sign of infidelity to God.

Yet it is the nature of humans to judge others by their physical appearance. Somehow we imagine that the wrapping paper is representative of the gift inside. If we are pretty, we are pleasing to God, we assume. But nothing could be further from the truth. "The LORD does not look at the things man looks at. Man looks at the outward appearance, but the LORD looks at the heart" (1 Samuel 16:7). "Stop judging by mere appearance, and make a right judgment" (John 7:24). "You are looking only on the surface of things" (2 Corinthians 10:7).

The prophet Isaiah recognized this human dilemma and reminded the expectant children of Israel that the coming Messiah would Himself be unattractive by human standards. "He had no beauty or majesty to attract us to him, nothing in his appearance that we should desire him" (Isaiah 53:2). Yet in our paganlike way, we recreate God in our own image. We make Him soft-skinned and handsome, often with white skin and blue eyes. We make him average height and weight with normal features. With a haircut and a business suit, He could sit in the boardroom next to the CEO. But if Jesus returned in the flesh today and was short, a little overweight, black- or brown-skinned, had large ears or had a mole on His face, would we recognize Him? There was simply nothing about Jesus's appearance that caused others to follow Him.

Nor was there any unique appearance that mattered in His choosing of the disciples. The ragtag disciples were fishermen, tax collectors, and common men, all chosen to be the progenitors of truth across the world. Jesus's words and relationships confirmed the value He gave to those on the fringes of society. The immoral prostitute, the despised tax collector, the wild-eyed demoniac, the beggars, the lepers, the half-breeds, the old widows, the poor, the blind, the deaf, and the lame were His daily acquaintances. The religious leaders rejected these troll-like people, except as needed for their own attention. Jesus announced that the "least of these" hungry, thirsty, imprisoned, sick, stranger, and naked were His representatives and caring for their needs was tantamount to caring for God Himself (Matthew 25:31–46). To reject the rejected is not right in God's kingdom. No smells, appearance, moral depravity, or economic condition was worthy of turning them away. Alternately, part of what it means to be in the kingdom is to have relationships with the least ones. The *ptochos* (poor) in Luke's Gospel represent all the disadvantaged of society and (says David J. Bosch in *Transforming Mission*), "the rich (*plousios*) are primarily those who are greedy and exploit the poor, who are so bent on money making that they do not even allow themselves the time to accept an invitation to a banquet (Luke 14:18ff.), who do not notice the Lazarus at their gate (Luke 16:20), who conduct a hedonistic lifestyle and are choked by cares about those very riches (Luke 8:14)." Jesus reminded His followers that His very mission was to "preach good news to the poor" (Luke 4:18), a clarion fulfillment of Isaiah's prophecy (Isaiah 61:1ff.) that validated His messiahship to John the Baptist and others. Using Jubilee language (Leviticus 25), Jesus reminds the rich that giving up a significant portion of their wealth and canceling debt, as exhibited by Zacchaeus after his conversion, was in keeping with repentance.

> Jesus's words and relationships confirmed the value He gave to those on the fringes of society.

The apostle Paul also knew firsthand how supposed truth seekers prefer the handsome dispensers of truth instead of the truth itself. Some Bible scholars suggest that Paul's personal appearance was somewhat repulsive. They claim he was somewhat disfigured or that his eyesight was failing, and still others think his "thorn in the flesh" was a disease such as epilepsy or severe respiratory illness. But whatever it was, Paul was certainly not humanly attractive. Ironically, when the false teachers challenged him in Jerusalem, Paul's own words indicate that external appearance was a factor in their challenge. "God does not judge by external appearance" (Galatians 2:6), he proclaimed, and pointed to his vocational call as the measure of his acceptance by God and His followers.

pretty people and the uncompromising gospel

Research continues to show that men and women and boys and girls who are identified as pretty, handsome, or cute are given special privilege in our culture. No surprise there. The dilemma for Christians is that this value has nothing to do with the kingdom of God. Not only are disciples of Jesus not to regard another's looks as important, Paul's plea for modesty would suggest that we should not attempt to draw attention to ourselves based on physical appearance. The Christian virtue of modesty suggests that we are to blend into the cultural norms. Overdressing or underdressing bring notice to our external appearance and cloud the beauty of character. Yet the advertising industry has seduced us to believe that the designer label, the stylish attire, the showy jewelry, and the revealing swimsuit are worthy objectives. The mass marketing of Christian jewelry and clothing lines merely compounds the challenge.

"Wear your best for God," was the norm for church folks when I was a child. At age ten, living in the record humidity of southeast Texas, I remember the misery of wearing a clip-on tie and a sports coat in the blazing summer heat on the way to church. Although today many churches have loosened their dress codes, there are many congregations that still expect flashy suits, large hats, and matching shoes.

Worse still, the non-Christian world, which identifies Americans as Christian, is repulsed by the pornographic dress of our culture. I remember being in a slum in India, with only one television in the area, and observing a group of men huddled around it, gawking at the program *Baywatch*, then the most watched television program on the planet. Though they enjoyed the moments of lust, they would never let their own daughters out of the house in such attire.

Ironically, in the Islamic, Hindu, and Buddhist worlds, conservative clothing is normative in their countries. Yet in the Christian

West, large-breasted women adorned with gold crosses on their plunging necklines are considered attractive and acceptable. In our culture, cosmetic surgery has replaced modesty as the way to become desired.

church Buildings and other Religious complexes

The need for approval of our personal appearance is closely tied to our possessions. Americans seem to have an insatiable need for acceptance and comfort. Driving the right car, living in a beautiful home, getting the kids in the best schools, owning the latest gadget, attending the right charity event, and eating at the finest restaurants drive the lifestyles of the affluent. Unfortunately, it is usually the same for affluent Christians. While the Bible clearly confronts such greed, lust, and pride, rarely do we find modern followers of Jesus who downsize for the kingdom in order to be more frugal with their resources for the kingdom. Looking good in the eyes of others seems to affect every area of life.

Perhaps no greater public display of our sin exists than the appearance of our places of worship. While few Christians still defend the church building as God's house, the vulgar use of excessive resources to build religious complexes for a few hours a week continues. Confronted with the reality that the average church today continues to give less and less to the poor and needy and spend more and more on themselves, there seems to be little repentance based on each year's growing budget to rearrange the priorities. Based on most current data, churches in America today spend less than 1 percent of their annual budget on the needs of the poor and hungry of our nation and world. Even among those members who become aware and convicted of this embarrassing disparity, few, if any, are willing to bring it to the church's attention in those business meetings where budgets and buildings are discussed. Benign neglect becomes the modus operandi for fear that others might point at our own hypocrisy. "We need an attractive and comfortable building to attract the unchurched in our community," the argument goes. We ignore the basic issue that the values of the kingdom preached and lived among the churched folks should be significantly different from the lives of the unchurched they are hoping to reach. American Christians spend millions on looking good, while the world's poor go hungry, with no apparent conviction that the two are related.

Trolls and the Kingdom

Kruger's simple, blunt question about appearance gets at the core of how the poor and marginalized question the faith of middle-class Christianity. If appearance does not matter to God, why does it continue to be a high value among His people? Why do pastors and Sunday School teachers not openly condemn our vulgar preoccupation with looking good and the millions of dollars spent to satisfy the shallow need? Who in the congregation will dare to stand in the business meeting and question the use of tithes and offerings for stained glass windows and immaculate lawns while a world goes hungry? And while appearance is clearly the symptom of the deeper issue, it is one of the topics which Jesus and His followers recognized as primary to deal with more significant issues. Until Christians can comfortably sit next to the Krugers of life and worship God with only celebration of the oneness of being in the family of God together, they are missing the joys of Christian fellowship. Hands lifted together, with fingernails both manicured and grease-laden, are a testimony that appearance does not matter.

The fact that we do segregate around issues of appearance keeps the very people Jesus sought out of our churches. When surveyed as to why folks do not go to church, the poor and marginalized list clothes as the number one reason. "It would be difficult to overemphasize the intensity of the issue of clothing in relationship to comments about why the hard living do not go to church," says Tex Sample in *Hard Living People and Mainstream Christians.* Proper attire and church have become so intertwined in many circles that it is better not to go than to go underdressed. Add the challenges of personal hygiene, haircuts, and clean clothes, and the barriers grow.

To give value based on God's image, not appearance, to the powerless and troll-like underclass birthed an "interim eschatological community" wherein the church models the kingdom to come "on earth as it is in heaven." These called-out ones who follow Jesus committed themselves to a higher ethic

proper attire and church have become so intertwined in many circles that it is better not to go than to go underdressed.

of love in which Jew and Greek or barbarian, male and female, rich and poor, and all colors and ethnicities entered into social relationships different from their cultural norms. "In light of this, any form of segregation in the church, whether racial, ethnic, social, or whatever, is in Paul's understanding a denial of the gospel," says David J. Bosch in *Transforming Mission*.

Kruger's appearance is a challenge to those around him. His long, uncut fingernails are laden with oil and grease from his mechanic work. His jeans are soiled, beard and hair long and unkempt, and on occasion his body odor is strong. He is, however, only one of scores of poorly dressed folks who attend Church Under the Bridge. There are tattooed bodies everywhere, and lots of missing teeth. One man has severe facial scars from major burns. Another has little of his face remaining after he attempted suicide with a shotgun years before. People wear shorts, overalls, jeans, dresses, and even an occasional tie. But no one seems to notice what others are wearing. It not a high value or one noticed.

At Church Under the Bridge, preference is not given to pretty people or dignitaries. The Scriptures are crystal clear about that. "If you show special attention to the man wearing fine clothes and say, 'Here's a good seat for you,' but say to the poor man, 'You stand there' or 'Sit on the floor by my feet,' have you not discriminated among yourselves and become judges with evil thoughts?" (James 2:3, 4).

And certainly the "church building" has little appeal itself. Located outside under an interstate bridge, the graveled "carpet," overhead noise, pooping pigeons, and inclement weather are hardly seductive in and of themselves to the churched or unchurched. Yet it is the commonness of the place that disarms the hundreds who attend. "This ordinary bridge made holy by His presence," points to God's ways when there were no temples and shrines. Like altars made by the patriarchs in the Old Testament from common stones and sticks in deserts and fields, this tabernacle-like location is mobile and unthreatening to those not ready to sit in a pew. There are no light bills, no construction costs (except to the state of Texas!), no utility bills. There is no need to be there, nothing attractive about the place, except that the presence of God is there. Financial resources are consequently freed up to share with the local and global poor instead of maintaining a building. And beauty is found more in the kingdom relationships than appearance.

Charlotte's Truth

Truth

put up or shut up

Change is not about words, but about actions. The Scriptures teach that a new mind and new patterns of living are evidence of transformation. Change is hard, but the church must.

our doorbell rang again, as it does almost hourly in our home of 25 years in the inner city. The woman on the porch asked, "Are you the preacher under the bridge?" "Yes, I lead a Bible study there. What do you need?" With tears in her eyes, she relayed the story of her sister-in-law found in a vacant field dead from a drug overdose. "She came to your church, and I was just wondering if you would do the funeral."

Her name was Dolly and we did know her. She came to our door almost weekly, usually black and blue from the beatings she received from her boyfriend. Each time we would bring her in, she was determined not to return to her life as a prostitute and never back to him. But the crack cocaine ruled her decisions more than any short-term logic and back she would go, at least until the day she was found lifeless and half-dressed across town.

The funeral was awful. It was a cold, rainy day in the pauper cemetery with a sordid crowd of onlookers unsure of what to say and how to react. Most had used Dolly or drugged with her and likely wondered how God would deal with them when their time came. Scripture passages read of a future hope of glory and a caring God somehow seemed as cold as the tiny marble footstone marking her birth and death years.

Charlotte, Dolly's sister; Charlotte's live-in boyfriend, Rusty; and their new baby stood among the crowd. I encouraged them as we parted, knowing full well it would be the last time I saw them. But I was wrong. Three weeks later, all three showed up under the bridge. They sat at the back, smoked cigarettes, and headed out at the end of the service before I could get to them. Two more weeks passed. There again on the back row of the metal chairs they sat. My wife got to them and gave a quick hug to Charlotte, assuring her she was welcome in this place.

Over the next few months, they came more and more, each time moving closer to the front of the rows of chairs. Through Charlotte's eyes of passion and struggle, you could see God bursting through her pain with a love she had never known. Within a year, she and Rusty submitted to that irresistible love and chose to follow this God talked about under the bridge.

What followed was nothing less than transformation. Still using drugs at the time of her conversion, still living with her boyfriend, and still caught in broken family relationships, Charlotte continued to listen and obey the inner voice of the God that she heard first at the graveside. Slowly the cocoonlike threads unwrapped the captive butterfly inside. Charlotte went cold turkey and quit the drug use. Her suppliers knew she would be back. But she never came, at least not for a while. Submerged in Bible study, prayer, and new relationships, her highs were now deep and meaningful. Together with her new friend, Janet, Charlotte returned to the trailer park and the crack houses she frequented. This time instead of money to purchase her former drugs of choice, she had her new Bible and several helium balloons. At each site of her dark past, the two of them read a Scripture and released a balloon, a symbol of the past now vanishing into the sky. While tears of joy filled their eyes, dealers peeked from behind covered windows and wondered what had just happened.

There have been more joys since then. After the Sunday worship service ended a few months later, Charlotte and Rusty stood at the front of the church. With joyful passing, they repeated vows of commitment in marriage to each other, and the church threw rice and celebrated a covenant love that has matured through these years.

She was subsequently hired by a Christian nonprofit, called Mission Waco, to run a thrift store, her first real job. Within a few years, Charlotte advanced to become the director of their walk-in center to help hundreds of other people in need with basic necessities. No one could be better suited for the job. She had been there on the streets and she could intuitively sense who was "frontin'" and who needed to be confronted. She is an in-your-face kind of lover of people who knows that the blunt truth is what most of those who are running from God and personal responsibility need to hear.

Still more change. Charlotte had been exposed in her new church to a wider world of missions that she only knew about through books and television. Ready to see the work of God in other places, she saved a little of each check and went on a mission/exposure trip to Mexico City. There in the barrios of the world's largest city, she saw the overwhelming needs of the poor, the orphans, the street kids, and the addicted. She told her story of this God who brings new life and changed her life. She returned with a commitment to take her children so they, too, could be exposed to the real world and become compassionate instead of self-absorbed as she was in her drug days.

From the mud of a graveyard in Waco to the dirty streets of the world, the transforming power of God continues. Charlotte's life has been a living witness that the gospel does change old patterns, heal hurts, and forgive sin. She shares her life story some, but most people who knew her do not need the words. They see the life.

> From the mud of a graveyard in waco to the dirty streets of the world, the transforming power of god continues.

≋

praxis

Change is painful. It requires an incredible honesty and humility to acknowledge that the behavior of the past must be replaced with new patterns of life. Yet as a "dog returns to its vomit" (2 Peter 2:22), so often short-term intentions of change succumb to the destructive former ways of the past. Genuinely converted prisoners return to their jail cells because their faith was too weak in the world. Addicts who swore they would never return to their drugs of choice more often than not do. Women caught in the cycle of domestic violence, decide the next man will be different only to awaken again with bruises and cuts. Even greedy consumers convicted to destroy the credit cards and share their resources with the poor often find themselves back at the mall buying another pair of shoes.

One of the greatest freedoms of Church Under the Bridge is the freedom to be honest. Confessing their sin and their insanity for repetitious choices that only lead to unfulfilled dreams, these troll-like followers of Jesus tend to be much less pretentious and secretive than most church folks. In fact, the honesty is sometimes frightening. From my protected background, I still find myself startled at some of the confessional statements I hear. "I assaulted a man, Rev." "I've been on a two-week binge, only to wake up and not know where I was." "I went out on my old lady." "I spent my whole check on crack and lottery tickets." And the sordid stories roll on.

Yet even in their depravity, the beginnings of change are in the works. Without the gut-level, honest admission that sin is destroying them, the process of renewal cannot begin. "Blessed are the poor in spirit, for theirs is the kingdom of heaven" (Matthew 5:3). This first beatitude is there for a reason. Without the poverty of spirit that admits one cannot fix it or cover it any more, the human spirit tends to deny, avoid, and blame others about its condition. But conviction of responsibility is the platform that produces movement. The alcoholic who refuses to admit he is one almost never overcomes. The sexual predator who never admits to God and others the perpetual lust that drives his destructive behavior cannot get well. The consumer who cannot stay out of the malls will never overcome. Confession is basic to healing.

I grew up in churches that suggested that the sinner must change to come to God. Biblical wisdom suggests otherwise. The power of conviction does not belong with the pastor, Sunday School teacher, or Christian friend. That is the unique role of the Holy Spirit. Although biblical teaching and loving confrontations are part of the Spirit's work through the church, only as the sinner experiences the safety of God's love can they risk change. Vulnerability of the soul follows unconditional acceptance.

The work of the church is to love the sinner in such a way that he or she can find the courage to look inside and see what is really there.

At Church Under the Bridge there is hardly any need to remind our people that they are sinners; but there is a strong need to remind them that God has not given up on them. When surveyed, those who attend say repeatedly, "I come here because I am loved and accepted for who I am." And in that womb of safety, the still, small voice of the Spirit convicts and confession is made.

> without the gut-level, honest admission that sin is destroying them, the process of renewal cannot begin.

The Next step

Change demands more than honest confession. Many with addictive behavior can admit their enslavement, but a new mind and new patterns of living are critical for genuine renewed lifestyles. "Be transformed by the renewing of your mind" (Romans 12:2) is Paul's admonition. As a living sacrifice, "do not conform any longer to the pattern of this world." Break the old habits, change your circles of influence, and you "reckon dead" the patterns of the past.

Though empowered by the Spirit, changing old habits comes not from some metaphysical, outward experience. It is the work of the sinner. Superficial spiritual language, like "I'm waiting on God to change me," is usually a cover for an unwillingness to go through the responsibility and pain of altering patterns of life. "Sin no more," Paul says in his confrontational way. Stop the behavior. Change. Put up or shut up.

Zacchaeus, the head tax collector of Jericho, was probably the greatest example of such behavioral transformation (Luke 19:1–10). Once convicted of his sin, he stood and announced that he would repay fourfold to those he had cheated and then give half of his possessions to the poor.

It is in this context that Jesus announces, "Today salvation has come to this house" (Luke 19:9). Conversion was not just words of confession but included actions of change. In an evangelical culture where words are too often taken as the basis of salvation, we are reminded that faith without works is dead. "Anyone, then, who knows the good he ought to do and doesn't do it, sins" (James 4:17). "Let us not love with words or tongue but with actions and in truth" (1 John 3:18).

Our churches have gone easy on us by allowing us to openly admit conviction with no accountability for change afterwards. Reducing salvation to a single-point-in-time occasion, we ignore the threefold tenses of conversion. "I was saved, I am being saved, I will be saved." Our cultural bias to ignore the biblical integration of these means we are guilty of what Bonhoeffer calls "cheap grace." Zacchaeus's salvation involved both word and deed. Change is the stuff of transformation. Though relapse and sin will certainly be a part of our lives until heaven, modern Gnosticism, which divides soul and body, word and deed, and accepts a half gospel, is no gospel at all.

> conversion was not just words of confession but included actions of change.

corporate change

Individual duplicity has been compounded by the church's double-talk. While we may acknowledge the gap between confession and action in the individual, few congregations have been so bold as to openly acknowledge what the unchurched recognize is the church's hypocrisy. Trapped in worldly expectations and models of success, the church has lost its prophetic voice in the culture. As mainstream denominations continually lose members and postmodernism erodes the concepts of progress, absolutes, and rationalism, churches in America have found themselves no longer in the center of the culture. But this loss is not because of some profound biblical counter-cultural revolution founded on Christian values. Quite the opposite is true. To the younger, unchurched generation, the church has compromised its values and has little meaning in a materialistic society that devalues life. Amid our religious habits, there seems little of substance which addresses the growing vacuum of nihilism in a youth culture reared on relativism. To them, Christians are just religious materialists dressed up in church clothes and living like everybody else. And like their European contemporaries, these "post-Christian" crowds have left the church in droves. Some statistics suggest that in the West, as many as 5,300 Christians a week have walked away from the church.

Transformation in the church follows the same pattern as the individual sinner. Honest admission of sin and compromise are basic to change. The church must corporately repent if it is to be healed. Each congregation has the capacity to examine its values, budgets, priorities, and impact and see if they line up with the revolutionary church of Jesus, who refused to accept either the values of His culture or the religious piety of the synagogue. We must find room for corporate examination. Revivals and Bible conferences could be replaced with open dialogue and confession. Small groups and even Sunday School classes can become atmospheres where honest struggle is encouraged. Sunday morning worship services can highlight testimonies of fellow sojourners who are asking the harder questions, not reciting religious platitudes. Pastoral leadership can encourage vulnerability by their own personal honesty and struggle.

Yet in our fear of hurting the feelings of members who passively accept the mere institutional role of the church in society, we sell out the gospel and its organic yeast in our culture. We have silenced the prophets who stand as reminders that God will not tolerate our private piety alone. We continue doing what we did last week and think somehow this week will be different.

Behavioral patterns must also change. How the church spends its time, resources, and energy is indicative of its true values. Though renewal begins with confession, it requires structural renovation. Institutionalism has often replaced function with form. Sunday School, hymns, church buildings, and clergy have become sacred ornaments of this complicity while we deem work and recreation as secular and miss the holism of God's order.

Missions is not an action of a handful of global church advocates in a foreign land, but the loving drive of the God who is a missionary God reclaiming all of His creation from the inner cities to the suburbs to the ends of the earth. Biblical justice is not sending money to a hunger organization at Thanksgiving, but collectively working to overturn the systemic patterns that cause the haves to have more and the have-nots to sink further into poverty. Evangelism is not slipping a four spiritual laws tract under the dinner plate as a tip to the unsaved waitress. It is building a caring relationship with her and her family which emanates Christ's compassion. Worship is not lifting hands to God alone, but lifting the downtrodden and rejected as well.

Just Do It

Church Under the Bridge has not arrived. If anything, we are more and more aware of the gap between what we say and what we do than ever. But the freshness of honesty disarms any false piety and reminds us of the grace that changes us. Each public confession of sin and affirmation of God's power over it is a reminder of our common condition and failure to be all that God created us to be. There is safety in honesty. Charlotte was free to admit that she was a drug user, living with a man, and struggling with life. A church of broken people can find ways to affirm, not judge, her actions and God's grace to overcome them. Communion, even under the noise

> Missions is the loving drive of the God who is a missionary God reclaiming all of His creation.

of overhead traffic, is a reverent and powerful time of personal examination and confession. But the sending out following the confession has equal impact. Just do it.

In the chaotic organization of the church, there is still a sense of God's ongoing life within us. With no paid pastoral staff, no building to take care of, and few expectations to be "a real church," we are in fact a real church. In the confession of who we are and the commitment to examine and change our structures to be consistent with the gospel in the culture, we live in the healthy tension of becoming. The freedom to constantly ask ourselves, "What are we doing?" provides scrutiny of our motives which prevents institutionalizing patterns of corporate behavior which are ineffective or dead. We are free to change, become, and ask questions in this constantly developing model of wineskin. We are aware that how God has led us is not the only way or even the way we will always be.

Charlotte's former life was repugnant to most churchgoing folks. Yet there was room for her honest search within a body of believers that accepted the Spirit's timing in her life and knew that as God convicted, she was free to change. She is still changing. And her life of

word and deed has brought humble reality that
the power of the gospel is a transformed life
that lives out the truth.

**Trolls
and
Truth**

DEDRICK'S TRUTH
use your gifts

The traditional church has taught most people to sit and listen, not how to live out of their unique, God-given gifts. We must empower everyone to use his or her vocational gifts.

❋3

from its beginning, Church Under the Bridge has welcomed the marginalized. Believing that God blesses His church with the least of these sisters and brothers, acceptance has been normative. Persons with mental retardation, mental illness, physical disabilities, and emotional or developmental challenges are embraced as valuable people.

Though there are many examples, none is quite as noteworthy as Dedrick. Assigned to an independent living center, he showed up one Sunday morning with four other mentally ill residents who were picked up by one of the church folks. But unlike them, Dedrick was a ball of nervous energy stemming from a psychosis that even confused his doctors. He spoke constantly but so rapidly that his mumbled words were virtually unrecognizable. At record speed, he smiled, pointed, hugged, laughed, and flitted around so spontaneously that no one was sure how to respond to his manic ways. But he wanted to be involved in everything.

That desired involvement included a request to be on the worship team. Though Dedrick had no musical talent, his willingness to contribute outweighed his lack of skills; and the theology of the church certainly affirmed that everyone has a place. At first he joined the group on the lowboy trailer used as the stage as the bongo player, a seemingly right fit for his high energy. Though he never hit a beat at the right time as he banged wildly, worshippers could not help but appreciate his presence. He frequently would leave the stage and walk down into the crowd of worshippers midsong to give someone a hug and then walk back. No one seemed to care about his distractions and visitors could not take their eyes off of him.

Yet the more he bumped into the guitarist and rearranged the music chords of the worship team, the greater the challenges became to get through a song. Undeterred and affirming of Dedrick's role in the church, the worship leader found a new, less-intrusive avenue for his leadership. He was given an electric guitar to play on the ground below the stage and down in front. To him the fact that his guitar was not plugged in did not matter. With antics similar to a rock band lead guitarist, he could now stroll up and down the graveled worship space, playing his instrument with incredible passion. Each Sunday, Dedrick puts one foot on an empty chair and bangs out each song like Jimi Hendrix reincarnated. Incapable of being still in one place for very long, he walks up the aisle of chairs and looks and points to each congregant directly as he plays, and even occasionally stops to give one of them a hug. Every so often, he will lay the guitar down and begin mimicking sign language, as if to communicate with those who are deaf in the congregation. Dedrick will slap a high five or point to an open page in someone's Bible or even take the bulletin away from one person to hand to another. On occasion, he will just disappear for a few minutes and return with a cup of coffee, place it on the stage, and bang out some more muted music chords.

Newcomers sometimes gawk at Dedrick, unsure if he is really playing the guitar or part of some skit they cannot figure out. They giggle at his mannerisms, then seem to find a deep appreciation that a church could find a place for such an unusual man.

And he is very much a part of the church. From a weekly small-group meeting to the annual talent show, Dedrick comes to everything he can. He is a constant reminder of God's inclusion in the family of faith.

> They [newcomers] giggle at his mannerisms, then seem to find a deep appreciation that a church could find a place for such an unusual man.

The polyphony of spiritual gifts

Most churches today accept an active understanding of the gifts of the Spirit, those manifestations given by God to build up the church. The breadth of the lists from 1 Corinthians 12, Romans 12, Ephesians 4, and other passages are debated; but many scholars argue even these longer lists are not exclusive of other gifts. But what they all imply is that the Spirit of God has endowed every believer and follower of Christ with one or more gifts. These gifts have no purpose for the individual and are given to the body of Christ. To not use them is, in effect, holding back from God and thwarting the church. But most churches today struggle with the practice of the gifts. How does such a diverse group of gifts fit in a church?

"Diversity is not a burden, but a joy. Diverse spiritual gifts do more than make a community minimally operative; they are God's way of allowing us to experience beauty and richness in our life together," says Lyle D. Vander Broek in *Breaking Barriers.* More than individual musical instruments playing harmoniously together in a concert, they are more like a *polyphony,* a word used by Dietrich Bonhoeffer to affirm the unique sounds of the instrument which do not distract from the melody. Churches which learn

> To not use them [gifts] is, in effect, holding back from god and thwarting the church.

to affirm the unique diversity of the church and spiritual gifts of the various individual members create a type of polyphony in worship that brings music to God.

"Those people" are "our people"

Of all organizations on the earth, the church should be the most inclusive one. Jesus made it so. Going into the highways and byways, He invited the tax collector, the prostitute, the leper, the beggar, the widow, the sick, the criminal, and the formerly demon-possessed into the kingdom of God. Based only on the affirmation of His lordship and a repentant heart, those the status quo of society often rejects are the very ones who become kingdom representatives.

Everything Jesus said and did confirms the inclusion of a sordid group that few of us would pick for leadership or membership. His disciples were mostly ordinary guys: an uneducated fisherman, a tax collector, and a couple of squabbling brothers. He even called the "betrayer" into the circle of apostles and allowed him to carry the money. The Teacher crossed gender, racial, moral, and economic boundaries in His clear effort to include "whosoever" at the banquet table. Ironically, it was not the religious leaders He embraced at all. In fact, more often than not, they were the ones He chastised, called hypocrites, and rejected as having any clue of the Father's real business. Even more insulting to them, He used the "least of these" to teach the religious ones what the kingdom was all about.

In response to Jesus's rejection of the religious standard of the day, they were inflamed with anger that a penniless widow could teach them about giving, a sick old woman could be as important as the synagogue leader, or a greedy tax collector could be worthy of salvation. How could a half-breed Samaritan be the hero of a kingdom story, especially compared to the rabbi and scribe, who were pegged as the bad guys? Indeed, this revolutionary had cut them to the bone and challenged the foundations of their religion. Not only did He undercut their prestige, but He placed the trolls of their society in a place of honor.

Are Exclusive Churches Even Churches at All?

Few Christians would deny that God welcomes everyone into His kingdom. Millions of dollars are given to reach outsiders with the good news of our Lord. We believe in prison ministries, outreach to prostitutes and transgendered folks, Christian-based recovery groups, and the homeless of our communities. We send missionaries to other nations and cultures to spread the gospel. We love to tell stories in our Sunday School curriculum and sermon illustrations of how the most disreputable people come to faith and leave their sinful past. "God is God of all and welcomes everyone," we say.

Yet the peculiar irony of our inclusive statements of faith is that, by and large, our churches are clearly exclusive. It does not take rocket science research to recognize that most churches today are collections of homogeneous groupings of look-alike people. They are similar in socioeconomic status, race, education, and culture. They tend to dress alike, talk alike, and enjoy the same entertainment. And most all of them worship alike.

A few years ago, a church-planting movement emerged and validated what was obvious to most Christians—churches grow best with homogeneous folks. The less cultural distance one has to overcome to feel comfortable in any setting, the more quickly one will become enculturated into the congregation. Clearly, one of our human traits is that we tend to get along with people who are like us. Although some took the intent of these church growth principles to an extreme not intended by the founders, many church leaders found solace in these teachings, which blessed their alikeness. Some even said what most were afraid to say. "God created us to worship with people who are like us."

Some would not be so bold. Most church leaders, at some level, recognize their church's lack of diversity and silently wish it were more blended. They recognize Jesus's inclusion of the ragtag folks of His society and believe it is an ideal which may not ever be actualized. And as any strategist will tell you, when a church decides to be an inclusive church, getting there can be a challenging road. It is as if the tapestry of the church begins to unravel when the marginalized begin to attend. Founding families are threatened that "their" church now has ex-offenders, people with mental illness, former addicts, and people from "the other side of the tracks." Parents become fearful that their children will be exposed in Sunday School to bad habits from the children of these families. Deacons and elders worry that the church does not have the physical and social resources to help these new people who will likely not tithe or provide substantial offerings. And everyone wonders if these new folks will shout or raise their hands or act inappropriately during the hymn singing or the sermon.

The Gift of Discomfort

The reality is that Jesus called us to serve and include the poor and the marginalized not only as objects of our ministries but as brothers and sisters in our congregations. The social misfits, rejected by the world, should find community, encouragement, and discipleship within the body of Christ. They should fill our churches.

Immediately, we pull back from embracing this view because of the challenges it brings. The marginalized bring discomfort to our otherwise sterile environment. They often look, smell, and act differently, creating discomfort and unease. They can intrude on our organized liturgies, speaking too loudly or inappropriately. They may project nonverbal messages through grimaces or stares that threaten us. Their body odor may infringe on our olfactory comfort and distract us. They may even use language deemed vulgar or rude that offends those with rules of proper talk and mannerisms.

Though rarely sought, it is this intrusive

discomfort that often provides the most opportunity to spiritually mature. As our own pervasive prejudices surface and cause feelings of offense, anger, discomfort, and intimidation, we are then painfully aware before God of our own childish thinking and can confront the shallowness of a faith that judges others and refuses to overcome personal preferences or supposed rights. In the midst of the discomfort, we are faced with the privilege of loving others beyond our cultural barriers or at least confessing the struggle. These trolls sitting in the pews next to us force us to celebrate a Messiah who touched lepers, sat with a prostitute, ate with a tax collector, and showed us kingdom relationships far beyond homogeneous peers.

It is exactly this point that Jesus was making in His diatribe in Matthew 25:31–46. His pointed interrogative, "When did I see you hungry, thirsty, naked, in prison, sick, or a stranger?" is the cutting question that most middle-class churches

> In the midst of the discomfort, we are faced with the privilege of loving others beyond our cultural barriers or at least confessing the struggle.

must face. We simply do not see them. We have gone to extraordinary lengths not to see them. Some move to the suburbs or gated communities, some build walls and hire security guards, and others create more organizations or civic clubs of look-alikes. "Seeing them," reminds us that all is not well in the world. It forces us to either time-consuming action or guilt-producing inaction. Or worse yet, we cry out thanksgiving to God like the Pharisee in the temple courtyard that we are not like them.

The Mentally Ill

Serious mental illness is the leprosy of our day. Stared at and even ridiculed, mentally ill men and women walk alone on the streets of every city in our nation, looking over their shoulder and fearing confrontation. Illnesses such as schizophrenia, schizoaffective disorder, bipolar disorder, clinical depression, ADHD, self-injury, personality disorder, and other diagnosable mental illnesses affect over one-fifth of our nation. Yet rarely do congregations make room for those with SMI (serious mental illness) or other major mental or physical disabilities. Our physical and social structures within the church seem to blatantly ignore the special needs of those that God has placed all around our neighborhoods.

Besides those affected, there is often little help for their caretaking relatives, who spend inordinate amounts of time assisting those who need considerable help to function day to day. Even a few hours a month of substitute care could become significant spiritual refreshment to those in need of time alone.

The world is watching

The unbelieving world quietly observes the social patterns of the church. Though they may not fully comprehend the gospel message, they are astute enough to know that Christians proclaim a higher order of compassion and relationships than the world. They know enough of Jesus's teachings and earthly activities to know that He was an inclusive teacher. Yet these same neopagans often discount the validity of the church because they see little difference in their socioeconomic patterns than the civic club.

Dedrick's place in Church Under the Bridge speaks loudly to a culture of unbelief. It suggests that the social order of the kingdom of God manifested in part by local congregations is inclusive and has room for everyone. This inclusivity is more than tolerating or relegating a seating section for them; it acknowledges that God also gifts them with talents and abilities that can and should be shared with the church. As the Spirit of God transforms churches, there must be a social transformation of relationships that sincerely creates a place for all.

A church living out this new order of fellowship inherently becomes evangelistic to the world. As the early church experienced while living out their new faith (Acts 2:42–47), the power of the relational gospel brought outsiders into their fellowship. "The Lord added to their number daily those who were being saved" (Acts 2:47).

> The unbelieving world quietly observes the social patterns of the church.

More than the cheapened evangelism tools and tracts used frequently in evangelical churches, God uses dynamic Christian fellowships that supersede the culture with a new way of loving and living. In this growing postmodern culture that rejects technique and mechanism, the impact to bring good news where there is little of it will be revolutionary. To see the gospel being lived out is transformational.

REGGIE AND SALLY'S TRUTH

overcome Barriers

The church in America still has not come to terms with its own segregation and prejudice. The church must overcome "dividing walls of hostility" including racial, economic, cultural, and social barriers.

4

she placed the gun under her chin and pulled the trigger. Blood spattered everywhere in her small apartment room and her body crumpled to the floor. A horrible life filled with chemical dependency, shallow relationships, and broken promises seemingly now ended in a final act of despair.

Yet even in suicide Sally was a failure since somehow the bullet never found its terminal target. Rushed to the hospital, it was clear that if she lived, there would be permanent damage. She did live. But as predicted, long-term brain damage affected her memory, her speech, and her walk. The formerly attractive blonde would only be a shell of the woman she had been.

His path also was filled with drugs, sex, and crime. On a path of destruction, Reggie was another poor African American who hated the system and those in control of it. He had never had a fair shake in life. Barely getting through middle school, he struggled to read and hated the classroom where the achievers thrived. Work was no better. He worked in unskilled jobs at minimum wage, usually supervised by powerful Anglos, all who brought only deeper resentment. Finally arrested and sentenced to prison, an environment of hate and selfishness seemed to seal his character of bitterness and blame.

In the midst of his pilgrimage to a dark pit of hopelessness, the surprising light of the gospel broke into Reggie's life there in the bondage of incarceration. He joined a Bible study inside the common room of his cellmates. With elementary literacy skills, he read of God's forgiving and reconciling work and knew he had to overcome his hatred and anger toward those he had called "slave owners" before now. And in those days of captivity, the same God who delivered the slaves in Egypt led him to a new place of healing and trust.

As if written in a storybook drama, Reggie met Sally. There, in a Christian group for recovering alcohol and drugs addicts, this formerly angry African American man met and fell in love with this formerly hopeless Anglo woman. His newly found gentleness and caring assistance for her long therapeutic recovery was amazing. Her piercing blue eyes often seen staring into his were filled with deep admiration that could not be ignored by even a casual observer. It was true love.

Reggie could not hide his newly found faith and joy from his new partner. He shared with her how God had dramatically overcome his own anger, rejection, and hopelessness. Having grown up with both physical and emotional abuse, she desperately wanted to believe that anyone, particularly a loving Father, could be trusted to love her unconditionally. So with Reggie, she cried out in her despair from a

> And in those days of captivity, the same god who delivered the slaves in Egypt led him to a new place of healing and trust.

broken body and a broken heart to the same God who had healed Reggie's life; and Sally, too, found a peace that she had never known.

Reggie and Sally soon found Church Under the Bridge and knew it would be their home. Here, there were few judgmental glances for their different races. No one laughed at her slow speech and sluggard steps. No one ridiculed his reading skills or missing teeth. Here they could sing off-key and share their life stories.

When they decided that they should consummate their love in marriage, the pastor met with them for counseling and encouragement. They wanted to be married under the bridge where the church meets and with the people that loved them. Unlike most weddings, there was nothing to decorate this open "sanctuary" but concrete pillars and a graveled aisle. But few weddings were ever as pretty. There was hardly a dry eye among those who knew their paths to this place and now heard their simple vows of love and commitment to each other. He praised her. She stared deeply into his eyes once again. And with the final words pronouncing them husband and wife, the cheers and celebration began.

☼
ʙlack, white, and ʙrown

The wedding feast that day among these troll-like worshippers was another profound symbol of reconciliation that is still being lived out under the interstate bridge. Working through the challenges of race, gender, and class, Church Under the Bridge highlighted reconciliation as one of its nine core values in the early days of its existence. Judging others because of their income, color of skin, ethnic heritage, or gender would not be allowed in this place where the congregation is notably living out their byline, "black, white and brown, rich or poor, educated in the streets or in the university, all serving the same God."

Yet the challenge was far more than tolerating differences, but a commitment to assertively pursue diversity, understanding, and appreciation among the worshipping community. "One of the greatest problems in ministering cross-culturally is the strong tendency toward a bias in favor of one's own culture," says John Cheyne in his book *Incarnational Agents.* To be the "kingdom . . . on earth as it is in heaven," called forth a unity which would require being both visible and invisible. Platitudes

Reggie and Sally:
Overcome Barriers

and idealism had to be overcome with genuine diversity clearly seen by anyone visiting the congregation. Like Reggie and Sally's outward commitment and vows of fidelity, the church committed to hold itself to a similar verbal and actual outward sign of a reconciling community of faith, learning to overcome the disparities that frequently separate our culture. The church would seek to be a reflection of the people in the community in which it exists.

> The church would seek to be a reflection of the people in the community in which it exists.

And indeed it is. Although the demographics change throughout each year, Church Under the Bridge generally consists of the same income, racial, and gender mix of the local community. There are homeless men and women, university students, mentally ill persons, ex-offenders, alcoholics, African Americans, Anglos, and browns. Over one-third of the church walks to the bridge each Sunday for worship service, some coming from as far away as three miles. Others drive in from the outlying suburbs. Some are day laborers, while others own the businesses that hire them. They are truly a mixed group.

The Bible, Race, and socioeconomic challenges

The problem of divisions around race and cultural differences are ancient. Ethnocentrism and nationalism arise in almost every culture of the world. Judging others who are different is learned behavior, grounded in the sinfulness of humanity. God never intended it to be so.

Even in God's selection of Israel as His chosen people, the intent was clearly to reveal Himself to all peoples so that they might respond and "have no other gods before them." In New Testament times, race and class were significant factors. In fact, the early church's first problem was related to an issue of ethnic prejudice (Acts 6). Yet the followers of Jesus were clearly aware that unity around His death and resurrection surpassed any color or class divisions.

And they acted assertively to display that reconciliation. Jesus' story of the good Samaritan still bit at the feet of a culture that literally hated these half-breeds. Peter's remarkable revelation that God decides who is clean, not Jewish law, was revolutionary. The Galileans who remained in Jerusalem after the birth of the church at Pentecost brought early language, customs, and cultural issues into it. When Paul took the gospel to the Gentiles, it required the church council in Jerusalem to make a monumental decision that those outside Israel were included in the kingdom, a decision that left a bitter taste in the mouths of the Judaizers who defended their nationalism. As churches began to emerge after the dispersion of Christians from Jerusalem, more ethnic challenges arose.

The Antioch church became the greatest example, in these early days, of the importance of reconciling believers beyond cultural divisions, which were intense in that city. "The Antioch congregation lived out an inclusive table fellowship that emulated the social practices of Jesus," say the authors of the book *United by Faith*. They literally broke with cultural patterns and ate and socialized together. But beyond that, the church intentionally chose diverse leadership to guide them. The young pastoral team included Paul and Barnabas from the Jewish culture; Manean, who grew up in Herod Anitpas's court; Lucius, from North Africa; and Simeon, called Niger or black, who was probably a black African. "For me the principle is profound: the local city church staff should increasingly match the ethnicity, class, and culture of the church members," says Ray Bakke in *A Theology as Big as the City.*

Reconciliation is a major theme of the Scriptures. "So from now on we regard no one from a worldly point of view. . . . Therefore, if anyone is in Christ, he is a new creation; the old has gone, the new has come! All this is from God. . . . And he has committed to us the message of reconciliation" (2 Corinthians 5:16, 17, 18, 19). Based on the compelling love of Christ, the church must live out this new ethic in a world that does not practice it.

> Reconciliation is a major theme of the scriptures.

Minority church recidivism

Ethnic and culture-centric churches have been the norm for Christianity. For obvious reasons, congregations that build around shared language, customs, history, and identity have strong allegiances in the dominant culture.

However, underneath the common bond of race and ethnicity, there are growing challenges. While the media focuses on growing denominations, like the Church of God in Christ (COGIC) and megachurch leaders like

T. D. Jakes's Potter's House, other African American leaders acknowledge that they are losing their men and youth, particularly in the urban centers. According to Jawanza Kunjufu in *Adam! Where Are You? Why Most Black Men Don't Go to Church,* "The average Black Church is made up of 75 percent females and 75 percent adults and elders." Though no national research confirms those numbers, it is clear that the average-size African American church has experienced major losses of the middle-aged male and the teens in their congregations. Reasons vary, yet many males express dismay with the autocratic style of pastoral leadership, blatant moral hypocrisy, use of money, length of service, emotionalism, dress code, and irrelevance. The same issues are common in many mainstream churches as well.

The Hispanic explosion, particularly in Texas and California, is redefining the challenge of the church. In Texas alone, demographers predict Latinos will become the dominant culture within the next ten years. As a mostly young, urban, and conservative people, they are also struggling with poverty. Ninety percent of Latinos live in the city. In his book *The Hispanic Challenge,* Manuel Ortiz says, "Once they join the workforce, they receive the lowest weekly wages of any major group in the labor market, with Hispanic women reporting the lowest wages." Though many are Roman Catholic by tradition, the younger majority have virtually remained outside its influence and teaching. Cultural ethnocentrism, particularly for those who either only speak Spanish or those who prefer Spanish, creates additional challenges for churches seeking to include them.

facing our Racial Divisions

In their book, *Divided by Faith,* Michael Emerson and Christian Smith prove with hard data what most Christians already know, but rarely talk about. Racial, ethnic, and economic barriers still profoundly separate the church in America.

As a young Christian active in an evangelical church in a small, east Texas, town in the late 1960s, I remember with embarrassment the day rumors spread that the blacks were coming to our church and the deacons had been alerted to not let them enter our Anglo congregation. There was no way "those people" would be allowed in to worship with us. Having grown up in a racist community which required separate water fountains, movie theater seating, schools, and neighborhoods, it seemed appropriate at the time to stand our ground in the unrest of the civil rights movement. With a blanket of spiritualized language covering their actions, the Anglo church remained fearfully silent in the face of change. Few were brave enough to march against the nation's overt racism that had long separated citizens by color of skin. Most Anglo evangelicals recoiled at the leadership of emerging African American Christian leaders, like Martin Luther King, who called the church to a nonviolent resistance against bigotry and injustice. Worse yet, white supremacists in the hoods of the Ku Klux Klan and other groups emerged behind crosses and Scripture verses demanding continued segregation as Christian duty.

Sadly, it was the judicial system, instead of the church, that forged racial reconciliation in our nation. Children and youth began to go to school together, communities began to be integrated, and the workplace was forced to deal with its own prejudices. But the church passively resisted. Although local congregations still sing "red and yellow, black and white, they are precious in His sight," the reality remains that it has continued to be the largest voluntary organization largely segregated by race, ethnicity, and socioeconomics.

Unlike the ugly racism of the past, however, the church and the culture have resorted to what Smith and Emerson and others call "racialization." The term recognizes the subtle reality that race still affects residential separation, intermarriage of races, inequality, and personal identity. It recognizes that racial discrimination is generally "covert and deeply embedded in the normal operations of institutions," say Emerson and Smith. In America, black and white marriages account for less than one-half of 1 percent. African Americans still make lower wages than Anglos, averaging around 62 percent less. Even health issues are racialized with research verifying that African Americans receive fewer necessary surgeries, have significantly higher deaths in childbirth, and are more likely to be murdered than Anglos.

It was the judicial system, instead of the church, that forged racial reconciliation in our nation.

Yet most Anglos refuse to accept these discrepancies and conclude that racism is a problem of the past. Anglo Christians unfortunately share the same myopic perspective. Even with clear, biblical mandates and examples that people of faith are "family" whose values should supersede cultural norms, there is resounding silence in most local churches around racial issues. According to Emerson and Smith in *Divided by Faith,* "Religion, as structured in America, is unable to make a great impact on the racialized society. In fact, far from knocking down racial barriers, religion generally serves to maintain these historical divides, and helps to develop new ones. In short, religion in the United States can serve as a moral force in freeing people, but not in bringing them together as equals across racial lines." Separate but equal is still the prevailing mind-set.

The unbelieving world recognizes the anemic condition of the church, which passively refuses to recognize race as a "wall of hostility." "They're no different from everybody else," said one cynic who had given up on Christianity. And according to research done by the Multiracial Congregations Project, "Only five and a half percent of Christian congregations in the United States are multiracial, using the norm that less than 80% of a congregation is from any particular racial group."

Yet signs of hope are emerging. A few churches like Church Under the Bridge are forging ahead with creative models for multiracial congregations. The efforts go beyond integration, which accepts racially diverse folks in the church, to a sincere effort to maximize the strengths of the diversity as basic to worship. "There are plenty of white churches with a few blacks and browns scattered in, but I want to be part of a congregation that celebrates our oneness beyond color," said Reggie.

Circle Church in Chicago is one such church, and has made racial reconciliation a priority. With monthly "fudge ripple" meetings, African Americans and Anglos discuss separately and together the barriers which often divide them. Howard Thurman's effort at the Church for the Fellowship of All Peoples in San Francisco established a Presbyterian model. Pentecostals, Catholics, and other denominations have made intentional efforts in some of their churches to become more multiracial.

facing our socioeconomic Barriers

Perhaps just as pervasive as the racial barrier is the socioeconomic divide. The rich and poor rarely join the same church. Economic class and social background are clearly major distinguishing marks in most congregations. Kruger discovered the walls of indifference and rejection, based on income, dress, social manners, and academic achievement, are high barriers to climb.

The biblical writers, however, would never accept such divisions. David J. Bosch, in his book *Transforming Mission: Paradigm Shifts in Theology of Mission*, says, "The apostle Paul sought to build communities in which, right from the start, Jew and Greek, slave and free, poor and rich, would worship together, learn from one another, and learn to deal with difficulties arising out of their diverse social, cultural, religious, and economic backgrounds. This belongs to the essence of the church."

In *Hard Living People and Mainstream Christians*, author Tex Sample explored the responses toward the church by those who are often struggling with substance abuse, unemployment, personal hygiene, homelessness, violence, and raucous language. They are ex-offenders, bikers, hustlers, protesters, and "trashy" women. "There is perhaps no group so hard for the church to reach in order to involve them in the active life of the congregation. While many churches serve them, few include them in participating membership of the community of faith. They are seen as winos, or trash, or street people, or something else, but not as brothers and sisters." The "comfortable church" that occasionally has canned food and clothing drives can only be effective if there exists a genuine care and inclusion, not cheapened charity. Worship must cross barriers for those who are illiterate. It must be more celebrative, with music that is contextualized and upbeat.

we need them as much as they need us

Reconciliation is hard work and few Christians have enough conviction and courage to face the broken relationships of the past. Yet, as Alcoholics Anonymous groups demand in their Twelve Step program, overcoming in the present compels us to deal personally with the sins of the past. Because we come into this world without the distortions of prejudice about race or class or social background, Christians must admit that many of their own opinions have been shaped by non-Christian values and "spiritualized" to avoid sounding so crude. Admitting deep-seated judgments toward certain groups of people is the beginning of change. Yet admission can be difficult and blame or justification creeps back into the confession.

Doing something about it is even harder. Good intentions or statistics rarely change behavior. Relationships do. For the average Christian who is disconnected from folks different from himself or herself, nothing can effect change like a personal relationship with someone from a different class or race or social background. There will be a hundred reasons why that will not happen at all or why it may be terminated before the new friendship matures. But only as the sincere believer deepens that affinity will there be new insights and awareness that leads to repentance and reconciliation.

Furthermore, "I am more likely to have Jesus revealed to me and through me in weakness than in strength, sinfulness than in purity, or doubt than in perfect faithfulness. Jesus is found in brokenness. When I admit my brokenness and enter into intimate relationships with God and His people, I am less inclined to judge others' brokenness. Essentially, this is simply the practice of confession, and confession is truly good for the soul," says Greg Paul in *God in the Alley*.

Juan's Truth

Be a giver

Generosity is a gift that the church has lost in its own self-preservation. God's people must be a sacrificial community.

5

His Elvis-like hair and tattooed

face brought stares from almost everyone he passed. Juan was a schizophrenic homeless man unlike any other. He virtually grew up in a bar next to his mother as she served the patrons under neon beer signs. It wasn't long until alcohol consumed him as well. Though he worked hard and could save money, the binges grew greater and holding a steady job became harder. In and out of trouble, Juan had gunshot wounds and scars from wrecks to verify his street life. Somewhere in his early 20s, his disabling mental illness kicked in and the alcohol became another way to self-medicate. After his first disability check arrived, he got his first tattoo, placed right in the middle of his forehead. This American Indian symbol was only the first of many to come to decorate his face and body.

Wandering into Waco, Juan became a master "dumpster diver." While many on the streets knew how to find a few good throwaways, this man seemed gifted in discovering the best of the treasures. New clothing, jewelry, canned meat, and even small appliances and TVs were listed in his regular finds. He once was seen carrying a small couch on the back of his bicycle. And when the college students left for the semester, it was like manna from heaven.

The funny thing was that Juan enjoyed sharing his new treasures with others as much as keeping them for himself. Living on a fixed income, which never delivered enough to pay the rent and basic needs, one would think that he would hoard his treasures and redeem them for his own use. But such was not the case. He would "work" all day, and then make his deliveries to various friends in the early evening.

My wife has belts and necklaces, my daughter has electronic games, my sons have designer shirts, and I have lawn equipment, all brought to us by Juan from the dumpsters of our city.

⊙⊙⊙

stingy christians

I grew up learning to save money. My junior high job as the janitor of a local drugstore provided weekly income that I carefully hid away in my metal toy bank by my bed. As a young, church-attending Christian, I was taught the concept of the tithe and then, somewhat begrudgingly, gave my 10 percent through the weekly Sunday School envelope. As I graduated to a better job in high school, folding jeans at the franchise department store, the increased hours and income should have made the weekly dona-tions easier since I had so much more for myself. But with a new Volkswagen Beetle and a regu-lar girlfriend, these costs of living complicated my church philanthropy. Through the years, with marriage and four children, mortgages, college loans, rising insurance, and numerous financial demands, the tithe became a grow-ing challenge. "Can it be 10 percent of the net instead of the gross income?" I wondered in my complicity. "Can I count the gifts to other

Christian nonprofits outside my church?" Or finally, "God doesn't really care about the amount, but only the spirit in which I give it."

Over 20 years ago, Ron Sider wrote a book called *Rich Christians in an Age of Hunger*, which exposed and enraged many Christians. Sider's theme was obvious: While most of the Christians in the West have unprecedented wealth, over 30,000 children in the world die each day from hunger-related causes. But his later work acknowledged that even in our own nation, the rich are getting significantly richer while some 36 million poor (13 percent) fall below the federal poverty guideline. "In fact, the poorest 10 percent in this country are worse off economically than the poorest 10 percent of every developed country except the United Kingdom," according to Edward Wolff in his book *Top Heavy*.

Research shows that church folks are giving less and less of their wealth to the needs of others and spending more and more on themselves. "Suffocating materialism and narcissistic individualism have wormed their way into so many Christian hearts and congregations. The path of self-indulgence defies God and threatens democracy," says Ron Sider in *Just Generosity*. Various researchers bear this out. "Church members have given to churches a smaller and smaller percent of their income virtually every year since 1969," say John and Sylvia Ronsvalle in their *Christian Century* article, "Giving to Religion." Today, most church members give just less than 2.5 percent of their income to their local congregation. Most of that money goes to meet the needs of their own church, with well less than one-half percent going to help the poor and others.

Ironically, poorer Christians not only give a higher percent of their income to the church, but the actual amount is higher. "The most genuine liberality is frequently displayed by those who have the least to give," according to Philip E. Hughes in *The Second Epistle to the Corinthians,* in the *New International Commentary on the New Testament.*

The poor Macedonian churches were noted by Paul as examples of such stewardship. Based on Jesus's adoption of poverty that others may be rich (2 Corinthians 8:9), these churches had every reason to hold back their

> poorer christians not only give a higher percent of their income to the church, but the actual amount is higher.

possessions. They were experiencing severe tri-als, but out of their "extreme poverty welled up in rich generosity" (2 Corinthians 8:2).

Generosity is basic to Christian faith. Biblical justice demanded that the poor, weak, and oppressed be lifted up. "Whoever is kind to the needy honors God" (Proverbs 14:31). In the Old Testament, God instituted several basic ways of helping. Gleaning left the cor-ners of the field to be unpicked as a way to feed hungry people who gathered from the cor-ners of those crops. Every seventh year, debts of slaves were forgiven and they received liberal gifts with their freedom to begin new lives. No-interest loans were available for the working man. And the Year of Jubilee was a profound new economic beginning when land was returned to the original owner as a way of making things fair again.

Like the eighth-century prophets who con-demned the separation of covenant love and mistreatment of those in need, the apostle John said it even more plainly, "If anyone has mate-rial possessions and sees his brother in need but has no pity on him, how can the love of God be in him? Dear children, let us not love with words or tongue but with actions and in truth" (1 John 3:17–18).

government generosity

Most Americans are convinced that the United States government spends large amounts of its resources on the needy, both nationally and internationally. The reality is, we have the lowest per capita spending on the poor of all 17 industrialized nations. And while the government is not the first line of responsibility to the poor, it must serve as a catch-basin for those who are trapped without other opportunity.

Though private aid and donations to charity are noteworthy by generous Americans, the US government's generosity is abysmal. According to Ron Sider in *Just Generosity,* "We Americans enter the twenty-first century and the new millennium as the most economically prosperous people in the history of the world." Yet politics more than economics govern our aid to the world's poor. Although we spend billions on the poor, it is still small compared to what is spent on the defense budget, tax credits to those who earn over $100,000 a year, and "pork barrel" projects of congressional representatives. "USA's aid, in terms of percentage of their GNP has almost always been lower than any other industrialized nation in the world, though paradoxically since 2000, their dollar amount has been the highest," says Anup Shah in "Sustainable Development: The US and Foreign Aid Assistance." While rich nations agreed to give 0.7 percent of their gross national product (GNP) by 2015 to assist development among the world's poor, many of them, including the United States, are cutting back on those promises. Self-serving economic interests of donor countries and difficult recipient demands dominate most giving, affecting spending on clean water, health care, and education in poor countries. Food aid policies are often more about foreign policy than eliminating hunger. The astounding costs of the Iraq war alone reveal the politicized choices. Estimates of $6 to $9 billion a month was spent on the conflict, some $200 million a day. Some, like Nobel Prize–winning economist Joseph Stiglitz, suggest that between $1 and $2 trillion will ultimately be expended, much of it borrowed. The impact of such national debt will certainly affect our national concern for global poverty, HIV/AIDS, child immunizations, and other needs. "It is nonsense to think that a successful, holistic campaign against poverty will bankrupt the government," says Ron Sider. Adjusted priorities and policies towards the

world's poverty can have an enormous impact
on the "least of these."

☒☒☒

wasteful society

A few years ago, our family hosted for a few
days a South Indian family visiting our country. After a couple of days, I asked the father
what his biggest impression of our country was
so far. Expecting something along the lines of
our large shopping malls, sport cars, or nice
homes, his answer surprised me. "The size of
your garbage cans," was his response. "You
have trash receptacles in each room and they
are very large and filled almost daily. You have
a lot of waste."

And indeed we do. Juan's "occupation"
as a dumpster diver bears out that reality.
We throw away small appliances, furniture,
clothing, electronics, and even edible food in
astounding volumes. In our consumer-driven
culture, it is often easier to throw away something and replace it with a new one than spend
the time to repair, paint, or upgrade the old.

Cheap and available goods have triumphed
over a theology of stewardship in a culture of
selfish individualism. God's "cultural mandate"
(Genesis 1:28) was for humans to care for and

sustain all the "good" He had created. There is enough food, clean water, and resources to sustain life for all on the planet. Yet a materialistic consumerism distorts that concern for others and suggests that whatever one can afford, one can rightly have.

giving Leftovers

Growing up in Christian home, the cultural alarm clock to awaken us to the neglected poor rang just before Thanksgiving. As if from hibernation, our church groups began to search for a special project and a needy family. For about six weeks, we collected canned goods, clothing, and money for the poor in our community.

But I still remember that when it came time to select the canned goods, I chose hominy. I hate hominy and refused to eat it. Here was a chance to get rid of it. Surely hungry people could appreciate this detestable food if they were hungry enough. And then there were the clothes, mostly old, tattered, out of style, too small, or forgotten in the back of the closet. These were the donations I made to those who I thought could overlook the small hole or frayed pocket. And with a bit of philanthropic pride, I gave my goods and called it charity.

Years later, I recognized that charity involved sacrifice, not giving leftovers or things I did not want to the poor. It meant giving the food I like to eat or the clothes I like to wear or the time I wanted to keep for myself. In a culture of too much, it is easy to get rid of the leftovers, but to the Christian there is an expectation and privilege of giving that which I deeply value.

ᘛᘚᘛ

Redeemed Economic Structures Needed

The Old Testament standard of God's desire was clear. "There should be no poor among you . . . if only you fully obey the LORD your God" (Deuteronomy 15:4, 5). Yet the poor are everywhere. Why? Perhaps more than anything, the institutional church had created bondage of its resources and held the poor captive with their expense structures and systems. If a church is going to take serious the call of God to end poverty among them, one of the key factors will be to redeem the existing structures.

Church Under the Bridge has embraced such an approach. It should be no surprise that a church that has no buildings and no paid pastoral staff would have more discretionary use of its offerings. Even though the budget is small in comparison to more wealthy churches, the access to invest those dollars in kingdom work is unusual. Built around a theology that believes generosity is basic to faith, Church Under the Bridge committed half or more of its annual income to go out to those in need. Each month, hundreds of the poor receive financial assistance for utilities, rent, food, medication, and other basics through mediating organizations to which the church donates. Donations are sent to local homeless shelters, job training programs, and food banks. As well, funds are sent to Mexico, Haiti, and India, where the church sponsors workers and projects. Individuals are sent to urban training or short-term mission trips to other impoverished countries.

Although most churches are trapped by growing internal financial commitments, a generous church will find ways to renegotiate its spending patterns to become more invested in the needs of the poor and marginalized in their own community and the world. That decision will force hard choices and long church family discussions. It will mean giving up certain privileges and amenities that congregants enjoy and even sacrificing to raise more funds for privileges for others outside the church. It may require more volunteers to help instead of paid professionals to do the cleaning, mowing, administrating, and even preaching. But in the process of such sacrifice, there is a recommitment to the purpose and mission of the church and the teachings of Jesus. Some will not accept loss of personal privilege and may even leave the church. Yet if the church in the culture is not recognized for its own self-sacrifice, how should we expect the unchurched to understand an economic value system that believes giving, not hoarding, is the way of the kingdom? Only as we live out Jesus's teaching about seeking first the kingdom, not building "bigger barns" or putting most of our treasures in things that moth and rust will destroy, will they listen to the gospel we preach.

VAN'S TRUTH
communicate creatively

Traditional structures within the church often inhibit renewal. The "new wineskins" of the church should be welcomed as God's new way of communicating the dynamic power of the Spirit.

 # 6

police cars frequently

responded to the 911 calls down our street at the Stott's house. Another family fight was going on. At 16 years old, Van and his parents all suffered from mental illness and developmental delays, traits that certainly didn't help them process conflict. Ugly words often turned to throwing, pushing, and screaming. On more than one occasion, someone would go to jail.

But there was something about that overgrown adolescent that you couldn't dislike. His enormous stature, balding head, and single front tooth caused many folks to fear him. But without question, he was a teddy bear wrapped in drama. He was certainly dramatic, and each day held a new crisis that needed someone's immediate attention. His stories were whoppers, often bending the truth so far from reality that one could hardly believe he believed them. To hear Van talk, you would have thought he had earned thousands of dollars a day only to have some gang rob him on the way home. Or he would tell of having been accepted to the local university to study engineering on full scholarship, knowing full well that we knew he had dropped out of school and had trouble reading. At a homeless breakfast one Friday morning, he had a whole sorority of Baylor University student volunteers crying as he told the story of his best friend's murder on the streets of Austin. It never occurred.

At Church Under the Bridge, the older children loved him. Even though now in his early 30s, as if one of their peers, he would chase them around the rows of chairs, squealing in fear and delight. His bear hugs were welcome gestures of the love he had for so many.

In what was a surprise to most everyone, Van got married to a wonderful young woman he had met at the mental health agency where he was counseled. She, too, had a disorder. But to watch them interact caused others to believe there is someone out there for everyone. They loved each other. Even while sleeping on the streets and struggling to survive, Van and Carla seemed like two peas in a pod. But then the baby came and the harsh realities of their drama and street life didn't impress the state welfare folks. They immediately removed the newborn from the bedside at the hospital. Even with the mental illness, many of us thought they could have been good parents.

Van was such a regular at the emergency room, the nurses knew him personally. With dramatic acting befitting *General Hospital,* he would describe various pains and symptoms in his body. On several occasions, he would faint or have "an attack" during worship services at the church and the EMT ambulance would come and whisk him away while the service continued unimpeded. As in the childhood story of the boy who cried "wolf," no one who knew him believed he was ever ill.

That is until one day his father called from ICU. Van had lapsed into a coma with acute kidney failure and enlarged heart. This time was for real. For a week, his parents and new wife stayed with him in the hospital hoping and praying for him to awaken.

He never did. His death was hard to accept because we somehow believed he was still acting. Van was buried in the same pauper cemetery as the many others from the church, but his funeral was anything but sad. There under a tattered tent, over 100 of his church friends gathered with the family to celebrate his life. Unlike most scripted funerals, this one was like several at Church Under the Bridge. Scripture was read, songs were sung, even typical words of hope were shared, but the remainder of the hour was spent telling stories, laughing, and crying at the escapades of our big brother in Christ. It was as he would have wanted, full of emotion and creativity.

⌗

Boring church

Most church services are boring to the average person. Young children squirm, wiggle, and talk too loudly. Teens write notes and whisper. Adults often fade in and out of sleep, just getting through the sermon. What should be one of the most celebrative and meaningful times of the week usually ends with a "Whew," instead of an "Amen."

As Creator God, how He must grieve over our lack of creativity and sameness. The God who made mountains and oceans, flowers and trees, kangaroos and iguanas, and people like Van must wonder at our dullness. Somehow through the years, we have reduced worship to stoic readings, outdated hymns, and mundane sermons. And though these traditions become sacred to the die-hards, the unbelieving world is not very interested.

I cannot help but think that the scenes on hillsides where Jesus preached the Sermon on the Mount and addressed the five thousand would have been very distracting to the average church member. People moved around to find the best grassy spot to sit on. Children played with peers on the edge of the hill. Flies and bugs certainly agitated a few listeners. An old man with bladder problems would have gotten up to go "find a tree." And at least in the latter crowd, their stomachs began growling from hunger. There were no microphones to overpower the competing noises or ushers to guarantee quiet. It was semichaotic for sure.

Church Under the Bridge is somewhat like that. On any given Sunday, the weather may

Van:
Communicate
Creatively

be inclement and cause worshippers to huddle closer together to get out of the rain or keep warm. The pigeons, roosting above the bridge pillars have frequently pooped on the back row below. Teens pass a football in the back, while others sip their coffee and eat the prepared meal. A woman walks to the portable toilet. On the gravel floor, a homeless man still sleeps through it all.

Once the service begins, it is not uncommon for someone to interrupt the speaker, or for a man on a bicycle to ride between the stage trailer and congregation. At least three separate groups circle up in conversation and never connect to the service.

※

A Donkey and a Hog

Though experience, drama, and creativity do not automatically make worship worshipful, they do engage the senses and often create participatory worship that has much more meaning for the truth seeker. While this growing postmodern generation rejects meaningless rationale and routine liturgy, they gravitate to experiences that engage them through various art forms, discussion, and exploration of their faith. Movie clips, historic paintings, debate, skits, meditation, and reflection are finding new interest in churches that traditionally defined worship with a choir special, testimony, and sermon.

Each Palm Sunday, when the humble entrance of Jesus into Jerusalem on the back of a donkey is remembered, Church Under the Bridge finds a way to make the reality of that historic event mean more through experience. After the annual foot washing among numerous groups of eight to ten persons in a circle, each group then shares Communion. Both events together profoundly remind followers that Jesus not only ate bread and drank wine with His disciples but washed their feet as an act of servanthood. It is humbling to wash another's feet, particularly someone's with calluses, dry skin, and broken toenails. But perhaps an even greater humility is to have your own feet washed by another. It is easier to understand Peter's bold, initial unwillingness to comply with Jesus's request.

When these two components of the service are completed, the congregation begins singing the Michael W. Smith rendition of "Hosanna," shouting the words, "Blessed is He who comes in the name of the Lord!" They are handed palm branches and are instructed while they sing to stand in two long rows, facing each other. Waving the palms and singing louder, they now see a homeless man who has been dressed as Jesus sitting on top of a small donkey and coming toward them from the access road. Slowly, these symbols of humility make their way down the line of worshippers and celebration of the King ensues. It is a great and mighty activity which captures the basic character of the Lord.

As might be expected, sometimes the donkey does not comply so well with the instructions, especially when the throng of palm wavers frightens it. One Palm Sunday several years ago, the donkey moved next to one of the concrete pillars under the bridge and refused to move. Everyone thought their method would generate movement, but nothing worked. He was not moving then or anytime soon.

So as not to be outwitted by a mere beast of burden, one of the local bikers jumped on his Harley-Davidson with a sidecar, pulled up next to the donkey and helped "Jesus" get into the sidecar seat. With all the fanfare of a parade, the ancient King of kings representative rode through the throng of palm-waving celebrants on a Hog, the slang name for a Harley, instead of on a donkey. The Scripture had become modern and real to the crowd. Each year since, the church does a donkey run and a Hog run on Palm Sunday. And in one Sunday morning, more is preached without a sermon about the Lord than in many days where the words get in the way.

✣

scripture comes alive

Though certainly Van's dramatic life can be overplayed, the reality is that most of the unchurched or marginalized are not cognitive-driven folks. They are often poor readers and struggle to understand the Bible. They are also easily distracted in traditional didactic teaching or preaching models, the accepted norm in most congregations today.

As any good missionary knows, learning to contextualize the message of the gospel requires understanding the culture, the Bible message, and the best ways to communicate the profound truths of God in ways they can really hear. Regardless of how well rehearsed or delivered, all the preparation in the world will not communicate if the "language" of the listeners is not used.

In a sermon series under the bridge, the pastor chose to preach about the life of

Samson and his God-given power as he fought the Philistines. Knowing no one in the audience had a clue who a Philistine was, a context they knew about was used as a basis for teaching. As any television channel flipper knows, the World Wide Wrestling Federation sponsors action-comedy wrestling matches, using colorful personalities that engage the crowds as the protagonist or antagonist in each fight. Literally millions of Americans are drawn into the encounter and watch with enthusiasm, regardless of how fake or manipulated the battle is designed to be.

Using the context of a wrestling match, the preacher came out on the stage dressed as a wrestler, in an appropriate uniform but with long flowing hair to emulate Samson's trademark. The stage was set as a fighters' ring, and the card girl walked sassily around the edges holding up *Round 1* on her display. Samson went to the microphone and told the biblical story of how God had given him power, through his hair, to overcome the enemies of Israel. As round 2 begins, the card girl, like Delilah, becomes the seducer who tries to manipulate Samson into giving up the secret to his power. In the deceitfulness of half-truths, which most of our congregation readily identified, Samson hides the real source. When the Philistines, now a group of three other large wrestlers from the church, come onto the stage to overtake Samson, he handily defeats them and throws each off the "ring" into the crowd. Every eye and ear are now attuned to the sermon and the troll-like crowd pushes closer to hear the final round.

Round 3 is the demise of Samson. As Delilah, the card girl, finally tempts him to give up the cherished source of power, she lulls him to sleep and cuts his precious hair and imprisons him, all the while stealing his symbol of power given by God. It is a message that this congregation understands. Many of them have found truth and power only to have lust and trickery from the world steal away the new confidence in God and His liberation. There is a close identification with the actors who clearly display the character of a sinful and broken world. They see themselves in a context that is familiar.

Of course, the power of that story is the ultimate defeat of the Philistines as Samson's hair grows back there in the prison and he pushes down the supporting pillars to crush the enemies, even losing his own life in the process. The church again is reminded that even in our

Van:
Communicate
Creatively

sellouts and lost battles, God can still use us to bring glory to him in the end.

Such dramatic sermons are not used weekly, but are interspersed in the flow of the year. But more often than not, the skits, first-person monologues, and Bible-come-alive approaches engender more real listening than the best three-points-and-a-poem approaches. The problem for most churches is that they do not have the courage to try such methods and stay trapped in a communication style that is out of date for the culture, but somehow revered as more sacred. We forget that the prophets were often more like Van than not. Jeremiah lay naked in the street. Hosea married a prostitute. Amos called the self-centered women cows. And to a nation that had lost its first love, these communicators were commissioned by God to awaken the lethargic followers in the most unusual ways.

> we forget that the prophets were often more like van than not.

⌗

inclusive creativity

Throughout the year, various creative services are designed to reach a world that is generally excluded in most churches. Church Under the Bridge has an annual Recovery Sunday, which recognizes the significant efforts of those who have overcome alcohol or drugs. Over 100 men and women who have committed themselves to be clean and sober are applauded and prayed for at the front. Alcoholic Anonymous chapters, many among them who only recognize a generic higher power, but not Christ, are invited to the services to be recognized for their work in the community. Local treatment centers and their staffs are likewise invited. Testimonies of Christians who have been delivered from the power of substance abuse and made the one-day-at-a-time decision shared their stories. It is a powerful reminder of the work of God.

Biker Sunday is even more colorful. On a hot July Sunday each year, black leather and tattoos are the church clothes of the day. Area bikers and chapters are invited to roar their Harleys under the bridge to hear the testimonies of these "bad boys made holy" and celebrate the work of God. The local Christian Motorcyclists Association club will spend weeks inviting "outlaw bikers" who are not Christians to come and hear the stories of change.

Other forms of participation and creativity are used throughout the year. Birthdays are celebrated monthly; children play handheld musical instruments, and even march around the chairs during the song, "When the Saints Go Marching In." In the midst of the creativity, overhead traffic, frenetic busyness, and several sidebars of activity, there is no question that God is the center of the worship.

FREDERICK AND HELENA'S TRUTH
Have good friends

Edification is the church's role, yet many worshippers never feel loved and accepted by their own members. The church must rediscover how to be genuinely friendly and understand community.

He has every John Wayne video ever produced and watches them weekly. She is probably the sweetest woman God ever made. Together this couple, who both are mentally challenged, bring more joy and encouragement to the Church Under the Bridge than perhaps any other. Married for 17 years, their simpleness is a gift. Frederick notices the sound of each ambulance siren that he hears and prays for whomever might be hurt. Helena writes notes of kindness and buys small gifts for others. Each of them has a cute sense of humor that virtually demands giggles from listeners. Both work "special jobs" but they also receive small Social Security checks to maintain their little apartment.

Each year, Church Under the Bridge has a "variety show." Everyone in the church is invited to read a poem, act out a skit, sing a song, juggle, or do anything they think would be entertaining. Dedrick sings the theme song to *Fresh Prince of Bel-Air* each year, all in about 20 seconds and without one recognizable word. Reggie and Sally sang their own song, but she just mostly looked into his eyes while he carried the song. Some teens did a step dance. But Frederick chose the Elvis tune, "Blue Suede Shoes." With a broken guitar and a swinging hip, he was the hit of the show.

Their best friends are Joy and Curt. Joy was the volunteer director of a large hospital. Curt is a businessman. He travels a few days a week, but tries to be home as often as possible. This is a second marriage for both of them, the results of some wild lifestyles in their younger years. Both are middle-aged, good-looking, upper-middle-class folks, and now have a deep faith in God. They live in a nice neighborhood, have a ranch, and try to take care of aging parents. They used to attend the large Bible church, but began to question the emptiness of learning about God and not serving others. Like so many middle-class Christians, Joy and Curt had a "good life," but knew there was more to faith than the way they were living.

They began to occasionally attend Church Under the Bridge. It was there that they met Frederick and Helena. In what may be the most unusual friendship of couples ever known, the relationship became an endearing and genuine one. Every week for the last several years, sometimes several times a week, they go out to eat together in local restaurants. They talk about each other's days, ask some questions, tell stories, and evaluate the food. Curt gently reprimands Frederick for his increased weight and lack of exercise and he agrees to start walking around their apartment. Helena shows them all a picture she made at "women's group" and then gives it to Joy as a gift for display on her refrigerator. It's a drawing of all four of them holding hands at the zoo. Frederick tells them about the John Wayne movies he watched for the tenth time last night.

They are truly friends. They call each

other regularly to be sure everyone is safe and secure. They visit each other's homes during the week. Since Frederick and Helena cannot drive, Joy and Curt often become their rides if the buses are not running. Joy takes them grocery shopping and makes sure they are taking their prescribed medications. A few weeks ago, they helped them distribute the bread during Communion to the worshippers who came forward to remember the Lord's death.

When the state mental health system began to unravel due to lack of tax dollars, Frederick lost some of his few and precious benefits that paid his Medicaid and helped toward their rent. In his childish mind, he simply did not understand what his caseworker was telling him about the impending cuts and the impact it would have on them. Like a protective dad, Curt went downtown to advocate at the agency for Frederick and clean up the bureaucratic messes of the incompetent system. He was relentless in his effort until he got the demands he sought for his good friend. Without Curt, who knows what would have happened?

Joy now spends her days as a job developer, helping low-income, unemployed adults find work. Curt leads a Bible study for recovering alcoholics and drug addicts after business trips. They are always busy serving others and could easily make legitimate excuses for missing outings to the restaurant with friends. But somehow, in the midst of the tiredness, there is a peaceful exhaustion when they fall into bed each night, knowing that the Father has used them and enriched them through Frederick and Helena and others they serve. There is the picture on the refrigerator to prove it.

"ı call you friends"

Servanthood is basic to understanding Christianity. When we surrender to the lordship of Jesus Christ, we choose to become a *doulos* (servant), willing to do His bidding. In fact, the biblical word for *worship,* means to "kiss the ring" of the king with unfettered allegiance to him. Rightly understood, obedience to God is worship. Sadly, much of our worship, however, is not about servanthood, but about an experiential feeling that may make a person feel warm and close to God. Many sermons, congregational songs, and Bible studies are based more around enjoyment or learning than about consistent submission to the King of kings. Genuine worship causes a person to recognize his or her position of disobedience, rebellion, and apathy and recommit to serving the Father. Like the prophet Isaiah, we become overwhelmed with our sin and unworthiness and can only respond with repentance and then servitude. "Here am I, send me!" (Isaiah 6:8).

But Jesus upgrades our status from servant to friend. "You are my friends if you do what I command. I no longer call you servants, because a servant does not know his master's business. Instead, I have called you friends, for everything that I learned from my Father I have made known to you" (John 15:14–15). No longer a submissive slave compelled out of gratitude for God's love, we now get to know the King's business and participate in it. We become privy to His strategy, His intentions, and His methods. We become disciples who get to walk the dusty roads of life like the apostles with the Lord Himself and learn from that friendship while He forgives sins, heals, and overcomes in the marketplace.

serving soup is a step in the right direction, but eating together is friendship.

We even get to eat with Him. It is no small part of friendship to consider with whom we eat. The word for *fellowship* or *communion* is derived from sharing common practices together. Jesus ate meals almost every day with His friends. It is in these informal mealtimes that friendship grows, conversation happens, and bonding occurs. Besides His prayer in Gethsemane, the last volitional act Jesus did before He was arrested was to eat with His friends. It should be no surprise, given the importance of that Communion activity, that during His post-Resurrection appearance, He sat with His friends in the early morning on the beach and ate together.

Who we eat with is an indicator of our faith. While many volunteers in urban ministries feed the hungry in soup kitchens or cafeteria lines, a greater measure of our love for the poor is to sit together and eat with one or a few of them around the table. Serving soup is a step in the right direction, but eating together is friendship.

But who we eat with can indict us. When Jesus called Zacchaeus down from his perch in the tree with the surprising message that He was coming to the home of the chief tax collector right then, the crowd was aghast. They hated this cheating little man who took more from them than was required for Caesar. He represented all that unfair government stood for. But now this "revolutionary" was betraying them, likely eating a meal as friends. He "is a friend of tax collectors and 'sinners,'" they muttered (Matthew 11:19). And Jesus became known as a friend of sinners.

It was no small impact when I finally realized my religious pretense looked little like the life of Jesus and much more like a Pharisee. Discipleship for me had been defined by memorizing Bible verses, church attendance, praying before meals, some Bible reading, watching my language, and not getting drunk with my friends. Though I had read the Bible for years, it never really hit me that Jesus, God in the flesh, hung out among prostitutes, lepers, tax collectors, and beggars. Or that "He had no place to lay his head," suggesting that God incarnate was in fact homeless at times. God's invasion into time and space was vulgar to religious people, who dressed right, acted right, and played by society's rules. But Jesus did not. As a friend of sinners, he identified with, ate with, and touched the culture's rejected ones.

> As a friend of sinners, He [Jesus] identified with, ate with, and touched the culture's rejected ones.

What must happen in our churches to accept such behavior as normal, not exceptional? What must happen in our fellowships to encourage eating a meal with someone who is mentally ill, is mentally challenged, is in a different economic class, is of a different color skin, or is morally deficient? When will we have the courage to condemn like Jesus did our own Pharisee-like behaviors as whitewashed impotent religion?

Ironically, friendship turns back to servanthood again. During the Last Supper of our Lord, "he got up from the meal, took off his outer clothing, and wrapped a towel around his waist. After that, he poured water into a basin and began to wash His disciples' feet, drying them with a towel that was wrapped around him" (John 13:4–5). At the most emotional time of His life, aware of the Cross before Him, this Friend served His friends, even as a common servant.

CONNOR'S TRUTH
fight for the least ones

The church is called to address the systemic issues that oppress others. While many of us separate evangelism from social action, they really are inextricably intertwined.

8

He stopped for gas across the street from the underpass where people were gathering. His trip from Dallas to Waco was a journey of wandering and desperation. Life had fallen apart for Connor. From upstate New York all the way to Texas, alcoholism and loneliness were killing him and there seemed to be no way out. His plan was to hurry the process along and find an easy way to end his life.

Before he continued his final trek, he wanted to see what this gathering was all about. He parked his car and walked across the access road to see. "We're getting ready for church," said the homeless man to him. "Church? You've got to be kidding!" It was far from any image of church he knew from his past. Connor pulled one of the metal chairs from a trailer and sat down in the back, skeptical of the upcoming event. For him, church was a place for good people and healthy families, neither of which fit him. "Besides," he thought, "churches don't really care about the issues that affect struggling people."

To his surprise, that day the preacher announced before his sermon that a recent dilemma had to be addressed by the church. There was no homeless shelter in this whole city for the chronically homeless men and women to sleep. Connor had slept in plenty of shelters and knew firsthand that these shelters had kept him from harm and freezing to death on those cold winter nights. How could any city not have such a safe haven?

Using various biblical texts, a message from the preacher about God's call to social action followed. "Justice for the poor and marginalized is basic to Christian faith," the speaker said.

"Loving God and ignoring the needs of those who sleep in abandoned houses and vacant fields is inconsistent" (see 1 John 3:17–18). "Do not merely listen to the word, and so deceive yourselves. Do what it says" (James 1:22). And with a strong appeal to the congregation, he said, "It's time to act. The church must do something."

A sense of encouragement overcame Connor. Here was a group of folks who seriously cared about the poor and homeless and not just themselves. He felt a desire to stick around and see if he could help. But Connor knew his addictions excluded him from his impulsive desire to action. He was a failure in society and had nothing to offer, especially now.

The service ended and what may have been the last stop on his journey in despair was short-circuited. Someone stopped and asked who he was and how he was doing. The man talked about how his own life had been destroyed by alcohol until he found some answers. Connor had never mentioned his own predicament, but knew that God was speaking through the conversation and was providing a sign of hope. "If you ever need help, these folks can help you," the man said as he got into the van to go back to his treatment program.

And they did. Within a week, Connor entered the six-month recovery program. For the next several weeks of his life, he gradually came to terms with his life and patterns of behavior. Scales seemed to fall off his eyes as he saw things differently and with new hope. His transformed life gave him a reason to live.

Within a year of his sobriety and new life in Christ, Connor was asked to be the house manager of the transitional home for the recovery center. From providing accountability for the participants to organizing recreational activities for the household, his shy personality grew into a gentle commander of a household. He shone in his new responsibilities. Serving others increased his desire to do more. Slowly he assumed more and more servant leadership roles in the church, pulling the trailers, setting up Communion, and doing whatever was needed. From a gas station stop at the end of life to a Christian leader, all within a year, still seemed like a fairy tale.

But the words of the preacher that the homeless needed a place to stay never left him. He couldn't forget, because each day a schizophrenic man, who attends Church Under the Bridge and who had nowhere else to go, frequently came and stayed on his porch. Now it was personal. With a changed heart and a changed value system and a desire to serve, Connor knew something had to be done.

justice Becomes personal

It was a cold Sunday night when two of the troll-like men homeless men who had worshipped under the bridge that morning crawled through the boarded-up, abandoned house south of downtown. Like other condemned properties, dumpsters, and camps, any shelter to break the wind was a worthy find. The men lit a candle for light and talked about various issues, while sharing a "40-ouncer" to encourage sleep on the hardwood floor. One by one, they faded off into a few hours of rest.

Somehow the burning candle was turned over and caught the dry wood on fire. Within minutes, the entire house was engulfed in flames. Someone called 911 and the fire department was there in just few minutes. But it was too late. Both of their charred bodies were found in different areas of the house, as they desperately sought an outlet from the inferno. Who knows what their last moments were really like?

Now it was personal for Connor. Standing at the pauper cemetery at the gravesites of these men brought a stinging anger. Regardless of what they had been doing before or inside the house, the reality that the community had not provided a safe haven for the chronically homeless to sleep made no sense. And it could be so no longer. He made a decision that he would join any effort to create a safe haven for people like himself. "How could any serious Christian not care about such human tragedy and need?" he thought.

With permission from the bivocational pastors' board of directors, a local Christian nonprofit called Mission Waco took on the project no one else seemed to want. Creating a homeless shelter didn't fall within their mission, which was to provide development programs instead of relief services. But these deaths left no room for clarifying the gray lines between relief and development. No one else should ever have to die simply because there was no place to find a safe bed. So the campaign began to find a place and raise the funds.

A local businessman read the story in the newspaper and volunteered $100,000 if the funds could be matched locally. A musician initiated a concert in the park to raise dollars. Individuals gave as they had resources. One elderly woman from an outlying community gave a dollar a month from her fixed income. Others saved coins, held garage sales, and gave up birthday gifts for the cause. Gradually, the amount grew closer to the goal. Then, unexpectedly, a local Christian philanthropist found out about a downtown church building being sold and gave the entire amount to Mission Waco to purchase the facility. With a building and money, the shelter seemed to be a given.

Though earlier assured by city planners that there should be no problem with zoning issues when they were ready to remodel the building into a shelter, such was not the case. The NIMBY (not in my backyard) effect emerged when a handful of area businesses and residents fought the permit, fearing such a shelter would hurt their property values and pose dangers in the neighborhood. The Building Standards Committee would hear both sides and make a decision, though it was clear that the appointed group was comprised of successful business folks who personally knew the complainants. Things were looking grim.

Church Under the Bridge was kept abreast of each development by the local authorities. When the big meeting was finally set, there was no question the entourage of "trolls" would be there. And what a night it was for

them. Both sides had their say. The rich elo-
quently defended their case for potential
property value losses in the slowly decaying
area and the fears that shelter residents would
cause problems by hanging around the facility.
Someone from the largest church in the city,
located directly across the street, talked about
potential danger to their children in day care.
"It will simply ruin my business and cause me
to lose all my investment if those people come,"
said another. A few boos and hisses from the
trolls filled the room. "Quiet," snarled the chair
of the committee.

With a three-minute speaking limit reiter-
ated by the committee chair, those who wished
to speak on behalf of the shelter were invited
to step up. Shuffling of feet and bodies simul-
taneously occurred all over the council room.
The homeless and advocates of the homeless
jockeyed for position and lined up behind the
single microphone, forming a line to the back
of the building. There was a pregnant woman
who talked about the dumpster she slept in
the night before. A mentally ill homeless man
talked about losing his entire business after a
tragic head injury on the job. The director of the
food bank reminded the committee of the dis-
proportionate poverty rate in our community.

A homeless husband and wife talked about living in their car for the last month. A local pastor and seminary professor reminded us that the people of faith had no choice but to do as the Bible commanded and bring good news to the poor. Then someone shared the story of the deaths of the two homeless men, a reminder that the pending decision had life and death consequences. Connor talked about his mentally ill friend who came each day to his porch. And one by one, some 20 men and women boldly reminded the committee of a world of people who were invisible to the community but hiding in the shadows of wealth and opportunity. It had been an impassioned case that seemed irrefutable.

Three hours had passed and the committee now had to vote. With the slickness of seasoned politicians, six of the seven made comments of regret and voted against the permit for the shelter in that location. The landowners clapped and shouted. The poor and their advocates ducked their heads in disappointment. They were used to bad news.

Yet the story did not end here. A former radiator shop, three and a half blocks away from the original building, was eventually purchased, zoned, and renovated into a 48-bed chronic homeless shelter called My Brother's Keeper. And the old, original church building became the new walk-in center where the homeless had to come each day to get their voucher to stay in the shelter and a place to do their laundry, take showers, and eat breakfast. Zoning could not stop that.

Connor had experienced the joy of being a part of an effort bigger than himself that clearly showed that Christians can make a difference for the voiceless ones. No more senseless deaths due to lack of safe housing options. And even his mentally ill homeless friend had a place to stay and was offered clinical diagnosis by Baylor University's doctor of psychology students, allowing him to get more help. This evaluation was critical in the quick approval of Social Security disability income, which subsequently provided monthly financial support for the friend. Today, Connor's friend lives in a mixed-income apartment complex of Christians and has an incredible support system.

Biblical Justice

Trying to remain pure, the body of Christ in America virtually cut off its own arm. Biblically and historically, the church understood that evangelism and social justice were parts of the same gospel. But at the turn of the twentieth century, a growing liberal contingency of churches began to connect with the work of Walter Rauschenbusch with the homeless in New York's Hell's Kitchen, and the more conservative church bodies pulled away, fearing an association. They turned instead to a zealous evangelistic movement that disconnected itself with social action. This "great reversal" of the early 1900s literally changed the nature and impact of the church. For most of the past century, conservative churches emphasized personal salvation with virtually no expectation of corporate change. Whereas historic movements like the Great Awakening and Wesley revivalism had emphasized confrontation of both personal and systemic sin, the modern evangelical movement, couched in the hyperindividualism of the West, concentrated almost exclusively on private faith. For the majority of the 1900s, churches ignored the injustices of the culture in which they existed.

Fortunately, in the latter half of the century, a renewed biblical understanding reemerged. Recognizing again, after decades of neglect, that the gospel was holistic and must include social justice with evangelism as parts of the same truth, churches began to admit the need to reenter the community with advocacy for the poor, assistance to the needy, and fairness to the oppressed. Slowly, churches have begun taking on new roles around the issues of HIV/AIDS, prison reform, livable wages, poverty alleviation, sexual exploitation, political inequalities, and oppressive child labor practices around the world.

A Theology of power

Many Christians immediately think of power in negative terms. Raised in a theology of servanthood and submission and living in a culture of frequent misuses of power, it is difficult for them to see as biblical the role of followers of Jesus using power. Individualism and "privatized Christianity" add to this tendency to avoid public displays of power. They often define good Christian character primarily around being nice. Though certainly Christians must seek peace and avoid unreasonable conflict, there is a time to stand against the evil powers that steal the blessings God intended for others.

Several different theologies exist about how God's created order became so distorted and abused. Some of these lean toward the inclination of social structures to become tainted by those in control who redefine them to advance their own causes. Others will lean toward the personal "principalities and powers," led by demonic forces to "steal, kill, and destroy" the works of God. "Behind the distorted social structures of our world, according to St. Paul, are fallen supernatural powers under the control of Satan himself. Evil is far more complex than wrong choices of individuals. It also lies outside us both in powerfully oppressive social systems and in demonic powers that delight in defying God by corrupting social systems that God's human image-bearers need," says Ron Sider in his book *Good News and Good Works.* Yet either way, that which is God's and created for His glory and purposes must be reclaimed using His authority and ways. Churches must help members understand the foundation of their fight against evil in society so that they may remain strong in the battles against the kingdom.

There is a time to stand against the evil powers that steal the blessings god intended for others.

Powerlessness is another word for poverty.

"Poverty is not about numbers. It is about inequality in power relationships," says Jayakumar Christian in *God of the Empty-Handed.* Christians are not only called to proclaim redemption to the captives (Luke 4:18, 19) but to overcome the marks of sin within the society in which we live.

And ordinary trolls like Connor, who thought the church did not care for those on the fringes, are hearing stories about congregations who are moving out into the marketplace and caring for those like his mentally ill friend. There is a quiet sense that this sleeping giant will awaken to more than involvement in extreme right-wing politics and the fight against abortion and gay rights. There is hope that Isaiah's words (Isaiah 58:6–10) to the self-centered nation of Israel about a legitimate fast which feeds the hungry, opens homes to the stranger, sets the captive free, repairs broken walls, and restores streets is emerging in renewed churches across the nation.

Beulah's Truth
when you're blessed, you should bless others

God's salvation and liberation are not ends in themselves. In giving our lives away we discover our purpose and growth.

9

NO ONE with that many problems should be so happy. At 54 years old, this African American grandmother was still living in the projects after all those years of dreaming for her own place. But things had only gotten worse. For years she had experienced the three-day-a-week trauma of kidney dialysis to keep her failing kidneys from killing her, but now there were signs of cancer. Tests and more tests. She was barely surviving on the small welfare check she received for taking care of three of the grandchildren who lived with her. How would she get them to school, fed, and cared for if she was admitted yet another time for her broken body? Yet she never questioned God. With a joy few Christians possess, Beulah puttered her motorized wheelchair down the streets of the government housing, singing hymns of praise as she went.

For years she had asked the Lord for her own home, knowing there was no way she could personally make that happen. Years passed and the cynics thought she was crazy to think about it. Then one day, she was asked to be on the board of directors for a local Christian nonprofit, which worked among the poor. Since most of the board members personally knew nothing about poverty, Beulah became the spokesperson for the poor among the middle-class members. Through the months of meetings and dialogue, she built a relationship with a wealthy businessman on the same board. Their friendship increased and his family began to visit her in the projects to help with food and basic needs. She called him her own guardian angel.

After three years of friendship, he requested

a personal meeting to tell her how God had blessed him to bless others. Holding a ring of keys, he handed her the dream of her life: a brand-new, three-bedroom house completely furnished and with food in the pantry. God had answered her prayers and silenced the cynics. Praises abounded and even the local newspaper ran a front-page story on the dedication day of this kingdom happening.

End of story? Hardly. What was her blessing has been used to bless others. Almost before the paint had dried, this trusting woman began opening her home to others. From women's groups and Bible studies to hosting wedding showers for other bridge folks who had no home, Beulah blessed others with her blessing. She began meeting her new neighbors and inviting them over for coffee. She rode the streets praying for others and asking God to bring peace in the neighborhood. She sang songs of joy up and down the sidewalks of her new home.

Two years after entering her new earthly home, Beulah entered her heavenly home. As the crowd packed into the small country church where she had attended as a girl, the homegoing celebration was just that. Black and white, rich and poor, young and old took their turns at the microphone to bear witness to how this poor woman with a broken body had blessed each of them. Everyone was amazed how many others she had blessed and helped in her life journey. And no one was sad that she only had two years in her new house because they knew she had just upgraded way beyond a three-bedroom, two-bath residence. She was now blessing God, face-to-face.

The purpose of Being Blessed

Israel's story is our story. It is the ongoing saga of how God takes us in our broken condition, sets us free, offers us a promised land of hope and joy, then watches sadly as we turn our freedom and joy into complaining and forgetfulness. It is the human tragedy of a people who have been given to so that they can bless others, thus proclaiming the power of the only true God. Yahweh sent Abram out (Genesis 12:1–3) from his homeland and peers with a new name and a greater purpose; i.e., to bless those that blessed him, that the descendants of the living God would be more than the stars in the galaxy. The children of God were to point to the only true God when Israel was blessed with victory or given favor, as if to say, "He is the reason, not us! Recognize Him as your God for He is good and His blessings go from generation to generation!" Israel was the evangelistic tool of God to negate the lies of the pagan pantheon.

In a highly competitive, ruggedly individualistic nation, blessing others is not all that easy. It is far more human to strive and win and count our own blessings as if we have accomplished them alone. Even in our philanthropic donations to the poor or social causes, it is easy to take the credit for amassing the wealth and the glory for giving to the charity. How quickly we forget that God gave these blessings and we are merely stewards of those resources! At any point, He could have taken these purported assets and the health we have to use them away from us. We quickly forget the support systems that provided the conditions that created blessing and opportunity and somehow think we alone were responsible for everything good.

> HOW quickly we forget that god gave these blessings and we are merely stewards of those resources!

Worse yet, after having been blessed, when things do go wrong, we blame God and want to return to the enslavement of our past. Instead of remaining faithful in the garbage pit as Job did, even through the loss of all his family, wealth, health, and position in the community, we are more like Israel, which forgets the brick-making days of slavery in Egypt and murmurs and complains along the path to the Promised Land. We choose to build our golden calves of personal idolatry and quickly forget the vanity and emptiness of these lifeless gods.

The church That Blesses

The church of Jesus Christ exists to be a sign of the kingdom of God in the culture in which it exists. It is the light and hope in a reprobate world that suggests there is an alternative worldview where giving, losing, serving, and turning our cheeks are higher values than hoarding, gaining, controlling, and avenging. The body of Christ is the visible expression of a value system that sets love and obedience above rights and freedom.

The early church understood their opportunity to bless others. They sold their possessions to give to the poor among them to the point that "they shared everything they had," and "there were no needy persons among them" (Acts 4:32, 34). The church has no biblical right to store up their treasures, especially for their own use. Blessing and sacrifice are the hallmarks of freedom from the enslavement of cultural hoarding, endowment, and memorializing.

161

Beulah:
When You're
Blessed, You
Should Bless
Others

Unfortunately, in the church of corporate America, we often describe a blessed church as one with the parking lot full on Sunday morning, a budget in the black, a list of new members, a good youth group and Sunday School count, and a wonderful pastor who preaches great sermons. Although those qualities can be great assets, a blessed church is one that blesses others, not one that has blessings. The church does not exist for itself, but only to give itself away as Jesus did.

There are two large churches in the same community as Church Under the Bridge that clarify this distinction. Both are from different, yet conservative denominations, which historically ministered only within their own structures. One maintains that same historic self-centered preoccupation in the local community. Its buildings are constantly improved for its own constituency. Good lighting, parking, comfort, cleanliness, security, and lawn care are high priorities. Each week it runs television marketing

> A blessed church is one that blesses others, not one that has blessings.

to promote attendance in its congregation. Yet rarely does it involve itself in the local community or the needs of other churches. Any giving for the needy goes through the denominational system and, not surprisingly, most of the unchurched in the community have dismissed this church as self-centered and unconcerned. A quick examination of its budget would verify that assumption due to a significant lack of support for local ministries or projects.

Across the city is another church which consistently blesses others. It gives thousands of dollars worth of food, clothing, utility assistance, and special needs to other congregations and nonprofits that help the poor in the community. From the time this church built its family life center, it was already reserved for outside groups who could not afford rent. The pastor leads a citywide collaboration of urban/suburban church leaders at great expense of his time and energy. Its members are on boards in the community and donate their talents for special projects. When the Hurricane Katrina disaster occurred, the congregation raised thousands of dollars for the special needs of the evacuees, secured apartments for those needing housing, and donated to a local nonprofit that helped provide job training and jobs for the displaced and unemployed. Though geographically suburban, this church is fully engaged with local urban churches and the needs of the community's poor.

163

Beulah:
When You're
Blessed, You
Should Bless
Others

Like Abraham's initiation to give his nephew, Lot, first pick of their resources, so the church must model blessing, even in the face of potential loss. Protecting assets and worrying about buildings and property are clearly characteristics of the pagan world, "For the pagans run after all these things, and your heavenly Father knows you need them" (Matthew 6:32). A church that is liberated to bless others with their resources, time, and talents is a church that has found biblical freedom. Like Beulah, joy and servanthood become by-products of that freedom which is not bound by the response of those she blesses. Personal needs do not give us an exemption from giving our lives away for others. At a time in life when her failing health could have easily turned Beulah's interest and resources inward, she chose to give her life away to others. So must the church of Jesus Christ.

BEN AND LOWELL'S TRUTH

sing wherever you are

The Christian life can inspire you to sing out loud!

Don't worry about the style of music, or even if

the singer is off-key, just sing your praises to God.

Music is one of the best ways for a church to

experience diversity.

10

Living in an impoverished neighborhood offers a host of unusual sights hidden from gated and suburban communities. There are times we sit on our front porch and chuckle at the wide variety of people, noises, smells, dress, and experiences right there in clear view.

One of those cartoonlike sights was first seen five years ago. An older man was riding his bicycle down the street on a very hot August day. The irony was that he was dressed from head to foot in several layers of brightly colored clothing, including a shiny orange winter cap that was pulled down over his ears. He could have been ready for an ice storm, but the temperature was over 100°F.

Over the weeks ahead, we would see this flamboyant man sitting on the porch of an abandoned home or at the bus stop bench or other places in the neighborhood. He was always alone and would, on occasion, take a small bottle from his coat and have a sip or two. On other occasions, the little man would sing out a popular song as if his audience was cheering him on.

At lunchtime one day I came home to get a sandwich and noticed a bicycle locked to the front porch. While coming up the stairs, I could hear singing from a strange voice and wondered who had come to visit. As I entered the kitchen, there he was, the little old man dressed in colorful winter clothing, singing to my wife! With the cutest smile and holding a cup of coffee, Ben sang "My Girl" with the clarity and passion of a stage performer. My wife, Janet, had stopped by the steps where he often sits and invited him over for coffee.

As it turns out, he had been a small-time singer in bars in his younger days in California. Alcoholism and mental illness had ended his career and he returned to Texas where his family lived. But his dual diagnosis and unusual behavior eventually estranged him from each of the relatives. He moved from rented house to rented house, living on a small government check. Most days Ben would spend riding his bicycle or sitting alone on an abandoned porch, dulling his loneliness with a flask of whiskey. Only the local prostitutes or crack addicts ever showed interest in him and their reasons were far from honorable.

But with his new friend, my wife, Ben established a new routine. Each day he would come to our porch and ask for a cup of coffee. She would bring it to him, often with a small snack, then turn on a CD with songs from the 1960s, all of which he knew by heart. Ben would sit on our porch for hours singing and enjoying the warmth of a new friendship.

Eventually, she was able to contact the right agencies and doctors, and Ben received the right medication and assistance. But it was not until Mission Waco's Christian-based living complex opened a one-bedroom apartment for him that he ceased his alcohol intake and found a larger support system to help encourage a healthier lifestyle. Today, Ben drops by the house occasionally for a cup of coffee and a few tunes from the past. And the best part is that he is still singing "My Girl" when he is alone or takes requests from an audience.

The Hills Are Alive with Music

Somewhere down inside all of us is a desire to sing out loud. Whether an old hymn, a flashback oldie, or a commercial jingle, singing somehow frees the soul to express itself and celebrate life. Unfortunately, most folks know their voices are far from professional, and they fear ridicule if they sing too loudly in church or break into a song in front of a peer. Public singing gets relegated to those who can stay on-key and know all the words. The only safe place for the novice to bellow out a favorite chorus is in the shower or alone in the car or house. How sad!

Ben, like an unpretentious child, naturally sings. It is in the heart. To not sing would enslave the God-given joy of life, which desires expression. In a neurotic culture which has turned to antidepressants as a primary coping mechanism to get through life, the simplicity of primal cultures which recognize singing as basic to life should inspire us.

Churches should encourage soul-felt singing, regardless of how off-key it may be. In fact, soloists without professional voices should be welcome to express themselves in congregational worship. Let the kids laugh when a note is missed. Join in when you know the words. Just sing praises from the bottom of your soul.

Better yet, churches should encourage newly written songs by their members. King David expressed himself in psalms. So should we. What could be a better worship service than a Sunday when everyone brought their new song to God and sang it freely as worship to Him? There would be no need for a sermon.

> To not sing would enslave the god-given joy of life, which desires expression.

Jailhouse Blues

Lowell was at the end of his last drug run when the police finally caught up with him. This time he ended up in the local county jail awaiting an indictment. Day after dreary day, he sat with nothing to do. His relief was country music, but it was hard to convince the other inmates to keep the television channel on a station that played music with twangs and steel guitars. But on occasion, he was able to hear, and eventually memorize, Toby Keith's song, "I Love This Bar." It was the story of a homelike atmosphere where diverse people from all walks of life could come and be accepted for who they were. There were bikers, short-skirted women, cowboys, drinkers, and "lookers" who all gathered as an odd sort of family.

Lowell's wife and six-year-old daughter had had enough of his errant ways and refused to allow him back into the home unless he chose treatment for his addiction. He did. Ending up in Mission Waco's Manna House, a Christian-based treatment program, Lowell was ready. He was tired of the chaos, pain, and running from himself.

As a part of the program, the participants attend Church Under the Bridge each Sunday morning. Lowell had attended church, though never serious about a relationship with a God who, in his mind, had caused so much pain in his own life. But he had never seen a place where such diversity and acceptance were normative. There were ex-offenders, former addicts, homeless, struggling families, and all colors of folks. Between his recovery program and an accepting church, he began to explore his pain and come to a renewed faith.

In the midst of those months, the church discovered he could play the guitar and sing, so he was invited to join the worship team. It was a perfect fit for both him and the team.

With Toby Keith's bar song hitting the top of the charts, several in the church recognized that the crowd in that bar was the same as the folks attending the church. After a little creativity, the song was redeemed for Sunday morning, now called, "I Love This Church." Words were changed, but the tune and essence were similar. In place of the "Mason jar of beer" phrase, it now referred to the "Dixie cup of juice" used for the church's Communion. Other words were cleaned up or put into context.

Lowell stepped to the microphone and to the surprise of the congregation sang the "new" song about a church he had come to love that took in all kinds of people who are often rejected in many congregations. The words stuck. The church began to sing with him. Over the weeks, it became the theme song as the crowd hummed, "Mmmmmm, I love this church!"

With the noise of truckers overhead, an ambulance in the background, and lots of talking, leading worship music is no easy task; particularly when the congregation is composed of some who like rap, some country, some old hymns, some children's songs, some Spanish, and still others the latest contemporary Christian hits.

But on Sunday morning, singing together is a powerful act of worship. Blending every brand of song, the church has learned to expect a wide variety of styles. The leaders on the flatbed trailer are as diverse as the songs. There is a postmodern looking man, "a long hair," two cowboys, a college student, two middle-age moms, an African American, and a Hispanic blended as one in their leadership. Children are often asked to bang rhythm band instruments and do hand motions while an upbeat song is played. The next song is sung completely in Spanish, with *gringos* trying their best to say the words. In the middle, Martin Luther's "A Mighty Fortress Is Our God" is sung by a

> singing together
> is a powerful act
> of worship.

congregation who has no idea who he was. "Jesus Loves Me" is a weekly ritual, sung a cappella with a sincerity and depth like few other songs. A hip-hop rap song will even make the cut. There is a violin, a bass guitar, drums, tambourines, and two guitars (not counting Dedrick's unplugged electric guitar). Sad for the old-timers is the absence of the scrub board player who moved away. Keeping true to the cultural commitment to diversity and a commitment to mission, the church will occasionally sing a Haitian song or South Indian tune. And "There Is Power in the Blood" is a regular "power song" on Communion Sunday.

contemporary versus Traditional

Most of the trolls under the bridge have no concept of the battle that rages around music in many congregations. Older church members may quit attending or withhold their tithes if songs are sung that are outside the hymnal or without the organ. Teens and college students, who may despise these old songs, beg for something upbeat and fresh. And compromising efforts to create separate worship services built around style, or other alternatives, dominate discussions in staff or church council meetings.

Perhaps music is the best place to recognize and respect the importance of diversity in the church. Most congregations need to recognize that many of their favorite hymns emerged from efforts to contextualize worship. John and Charles Wesley took the songs of the local miners and the bars and redeemed them into Christian songs that we still sing today.

One's short look at history tends to create subjective traditions that were modern and unacceptable when they were first sung. Much to the disbelief of some, "The Old Rugged Cross" and "Amazing Grace" were not sung by Jesus and the disciples, but written after 1,800 years of church history. To be a true traditionalist, one must sing in Hebrew or Aramaic, with a Jewish beat unlike few hymns. The church must discard the old, burst wineskins of "sacred music" and recognize God also inhabits the new forms of singing that bring glory to Him, whether in hip-hop style or cantatas.

ZEKE'S TRUTH

Dance a Little Too

King David could not help but dance as he understood the joy of God's presence. So must we. The church shouldn't be afraid of a little movement.

II

His appearance suggests

something physical or mental is wrong. One eye seems to bug out, and he walks a little unusually. Zeke showed up at the Christian inner-city free computer lab to learn how to work on the Internet. For hours each day, he plays computer games, searches for baseball scores, or practices his keyboarding. On his short breaks outside the building, he shows the staff members his long list of scores from the previous night's games. Then he goes down to the office and stands around as a doorman to invite visitors into the building or help them get donations out of their car. He is truly a kind young man.

Befriended by one of the staff members, Zeke was invited to Church Under the Bridge. Immediately, he knew he had found a home where he could be accepted as he was and not be stared at by others. He never missed a week and those on the stage never missed seeing him. When the worship music began, his energetic body began moving. Arms uplifted, feet moving, and a smile as big as his face, he could not stand still as he sang the new songs about Jesus that he had never heard.

Recognizing his enthusiasm, the music leader invited him to come and stand down front with Dedrick and help lead with his dancing and joy. If the song is slow, he may just stand and mimic the words. But if the beat is strong and energetic, Zeke unleashes his frenetic movements and clapping and creates a mood of celebration like few traditional churches know.

Neo-pentecostals

I grew up in a conservative Baptist church that put the T in tradition. The service was routinely predictable. We started at 11:00 A.M. and finished at 12:00 noon, hopefully before the nearby Methodist church, which often beat us to the cafeteria line. For some reason we almost never sang the third verse of a four-verse song. We always stood up on the song before the offering, most likely to be able to get to our pockets, but no one would say that. We wore "church clothes," read from the King James Version, and never clapped in the service. And we certainly did not raise our hands to worship. That was for the Pentecostals and we all knew how weird they were. In fact, as kids, we would ride our bicycles over to their little church to peek through the windows to watch them shout, raise their hands, and even dance. It was a show in itself.

We Baptists did not dance. At least we said we did not. We ignored or discounted the Bible verses about David dancing before the Lord, just as we had done with the wine-drinking passages that seemed to negate our antialcohol stand. Our Sunday School teachers had somehow explained that most dancing led to going to bars which led to drinking which led to sexual immorality, and we knew all those things were wrong. But somehow the connection between wiggling a little during an upbeat song and fornicating seemed a bit of a stretch to our adolescent minds.

We danced anyway. Sometimes it was the Saturday night dance for teens held at the old skating rink that lured us. But sometimes we went down the street to the Episcopal church that sponsored dances. The concept of a church-sponsored dance was way out of our theology. They certainly did not look Pentecostal. During Sunday School the next morning, we kept our vows of silence so the teacher would not know the depths of sin we had participated in the night before as we twisted to Chubby Checker or did the Swim. Occasionally, a friend would walk the aisle in church on Sunday morning and rededicate his life, confessing the sin of dancing and virtually implicating the rest of us.

Over the next 20 years, something strange happened to many of the "normal" churches. Some members began to clap in church after a moving song special or to keep beat with an upbeat song. A woman might raise her hand and say out loud, "Thank You, Lord." Some folks would stand up while others were sitting, raise both hands with eyes closed, and pray right there in the worship service. And in a few places, "real Christians" even danced.

To my surprise, their buildings did not collapse into a cavernous hole at this seeming abomination. In fact, somehow, it even seemed right to express deep gratitude to God for His unspeakable gift! Could it be that my own religious tradition had missed something that the Pentecostals understood? The mere idea seemed blasphemous.

Today, outward expression of thanksgiving and praise to God is not uncommon in many, if not most, denominations. Recognition of the Spirit's filling presence to honor the Father is acceptable theology to most Christians. This is not some "tongue-speaking, wild-eyed, snake-throwing, hair-in-a-bun, no-makeup" religion. With order and with freedom, churches have discovered that raised hands, verbal praises, and even some occasional dancing is acceptable to the Lord. Or one can be free to do none of those things and worship in silence and stillness.

Decently and in order, the apostle Paul

> Recognition of the spirit's filling presence to honor the father is acceptable theology to most christians.

reminded the Corinthian church. Cultural expressions of praise may vary in an African American Pentecostal church from a high liturgical Episcopalian Rite I service. Both can create a worshipful atmosphere, as different as they may be. But both can become entrenched in deadening methodologies or routine order just as easily as they can become disorderly. King David's dancing certainly was decent and in order, and certainly God must have been honored by this "man after God's own heart" who found it pleasing in the Lord's presence to move his body in celebration of Jehovah-Jireh.

I still personally find it somewhat uncomfortable to raise my hands in corporate worship, not because it is wrong, but because it is not natural for me. It is hard to overcome a half-century of tradition. I never shout or even say a loud "Amen!" Though I do clap on occasion, I worry that applause can too quickly shift the glory of a beautiful solo to the person instead of the Father. But on occasion, when the worship team under the bridge plays "Lord of the Dance," I must admit I do just that, but just a little. Please do not tell my old Sunday School teacher!

RUSS'S TRUTH

work for the Lord

Those who have been unemployed or underemployed know that work is a blessing. The church can help not just with charity, but by empowering people to find a job that fulfills God's calling in their lives.

12

AT 38 years old, with good health and a desire to be somebody, Russ could not imagine why he could not break the cycle of poverty which had taken away his self-respect. He had tried. In fact, he had tried a lot. He walked miles and miles across the city, putting in applications everywhere, just hoping for a break to land a full-time job. He continued to work a few days a week, in between his job searches, at the day labor pool. Last week was the same old rotten job, cutting onions on the night shift for $6.00 an hour.

On a tip, Russ heard about a Christian-based job training program which could help him connect with local employers and help with GED classes. He was waiting at the door the next morning asking for admittance into the next class. Bright and early on the first day of class, he found himself in the middle of a caring support system who trained, encouraged, and advocated for him. For the next three weeks, he worked on résumés, learned interviewing skills, role-played conflict resolution methods, practiced job finding on the Internet, and attended night classes in the GED program.

Within three weeks, the job developer knew enough about his abilities and character to advocate in the community for various jobs for Russ. On the second day of her search, the city offices said they needed a full-time guy at the landfill. Not much of a job, but it was enough for him to get excited. Monday morning, again, bright and early, he was on the job. Working among the community's trash might have discouraged some folks, but Russ walked or hitched a ride there every day, an hour before he had to be there. He made the coffee in the breakroom, picked up and straightened the chairs, and greeted the workers as they came in. His contagious smile disarmed the grumpy workers who could not believe anyone could be so friendly so early and at a landfill job. Out on the work site, he worked as if he enjoyed every minute of it. Even his boss was amazed.

To show their appreciation, the city workers pooled their money and bought Russ a bicycle so he could make the trip from the shelter to the dump on his own. They told other city employees about his work ethic and friendliness. So the city interviewed him and put his picture and story in their monthly newsletter. He had become a kind of model worker that brought respect from among his peers.

Within the month, Russ was promoted to the Parks and Recreation Department, where he continues to work. Now with a solid paycheck, he has rented his own apartment and bought a few new clothes. He still rides his bicycle to work each day and still has that contagious smile. And he also still works hard each day because he believes that's what Christians are supposed to do to bring honor to God in the workplace.

∽

get a job!

It is hard to imagine what a whole day asking for money on the street corner would do to one's self-image. Through the years, several of the trolls at Church Under the Bridge have panhandled for a living, at least until the city made it illegal. Hour after hour they would stand with their *Will Work for Food* sign in the blazing Texas summer heat and get an array of responses. A few drivers would hand out a little change, have a brief conversation, or offer some fast food from the seat of the car. Most, however, would either look the other way to avoid eye contact with the homeless man, casually lock the car doors, then speed through the intersection as soon as the light turned green. A few, however, would yell from their windows, "Get a job, you lazy bum!"

The modern phenomenon of homelessness grew out of three trends. First there was the major financial cut to most mental hospitals during the Reagan administration, forcing most of the facilities to turn thousands of mentally ill persons onto the streets. Those without support systems of family and friends often ended up under bridges and shelters of local communities. At least one-third of all chronically homeless persons today are mentally ill, without case management and proper medication. The swell of the baby boomers added to these numbers as more and more people demanded more from the social systems. And finally, the diminishing lack of unskilled labor jobs made finding any job difficult. The growth of day labor pools meant employers, who had formerly hired full-time workers with benefits like insurance, could get cheaper labor without any paying benefits. The days when a high school dropout could get a reasonable job and support a family were over.

☉☉

The Ministry of work

Almost half of our waking hours are spent at work. Yet the reality is few workers have a "theology of work." They just routinely get up, do their job, and go home. This *bios* (mere existence) falls significantly short of God's intended *zoe* (abundant life) filled with meaning and purpose.

Many workers see their labor as a result of God's curse on Adam after his sin in the Garden of Eden. But work existed before the curse. God had given the first couple the mandate of caring for the garden, naming the animals, and subduing the earth (Genesis 1:27–28). It was only after their sin that the ground was made difficult to work. Work is a part of God's created order. Doing something significant with one's hands is a blessing.

In the Greek culture, this was reversed. Work done by servants, the common folk, while the wealthy would retreat to the respected places of dialogue and philosophical discourse. No respected person would do common labor.

In the Reformation, however, Martin Luther redeemed the place of work. Until then, the truly spiritual persons were the monks in the monasteries, who lived outside the world and devoted themselves to prayer and study. The common worker could never be "spiritual" because of his plight of daily labor. But Luther gave new theological understanding to one's "station," or ordinary job. Instead of despising it, he suggested that this was where God placed His followers and the day could be spent honoring God through one's hands. John Calvin added to Luther's idea, suggesting that the worker should be free

> work is a part of god's created order. doing something significant with one's hands is a blessing.

to seek out the appropriate employment that best fit the gifts God had given him or her.

A new sense of vocation began to affect the workplace. Calling, not some miserable effort to make a few dollars, should guide the day's purpose. The goal of the worker was to discover the unique calling of God for which he was created.

The mechanization of the Industrial Revolution complicated a sense of joyful call on the job. Industrialization dumbed down many work positions to nothing more than routine and boring tasks. Workers spent long hours in large factories simply getting through the day.

> The goal of the worker was to discover the unique calling of god for which he was created.

The careerism of the modern era has eradicated some of this meaninglessness. With enough education and opportunity, students could eventually become doctors, lawyers, businesspeople, or teachers. To the question, "What do you want to be when you grow up?" most adolescents now think in terms of a career, not a vocation. Even Christian schools and churches have bought into valuing a title over a sense of calling by God. Most young Christians have no sense of God's calling, even though they may have a strong sense of what job they want to have someday. They spend years in training and thousands of dollars, all without exploring call clarification. "Who am I and what unique role has God put me on the earth to fulfill to bring Him glory?" How one makes money should be secondary or subservient to one's call. Many professionals today actually have careers that leave no time or energy left for their calling. They may have money in the bank, but the sense of purpose wanes.

Beyond charity

The poor have fewer choices. With little education or training, children to feed, and soaring housing and utility costs, mere existence is hard enough. Any job is a blessing. "The institution of work is undeniably one of the chief integrators of persons in our society. It orients our lives; it organizes our time; it puts us in touch with people. To be unemployed is to be afflicted with a kind of social leprosy," says Lee Hardy in *The Fabric of This World*. When jobs are not available or accessible, social systems become the fall-back opportunity. Extended family, churches, nonprofits, and government are the next lines of assistance. Once these are exhausted, often a sense of desperation moves some of those in need toward hopelessness and manipulation.

As important and necessary as charity is for the poor, it can also become part of the problem. Extended relief that asks nothing of the one being helped erodes his or her self-respect. The older welfare system, called Aid to Families with Dependent Children (AFDC), did more harm than most realized. It created dependency without responsibility. The biblical principle that a man who will not work cannot eat was not as much punitive as character-based. Empowerment to overcome demands a different approach than soup lines and giveaway programs. It requires jobs, education, adequate health care, and well-being. "For Christian development work to be holistic, we must work to redeem the powers to the point where they can fulfill their ordained purpose more effectively," says Bruce Bradshaw in his book *Bridging the Gap*.

While in Atlanta a few years ago for a tour of Bob Lupton's development work among the poor, I asked how much money his recycled home improvement supplies store made for his ministry. His answer, "Four jobs." Four of the poor who had been unemployed or underemployed now had good, full-time jobs with benefits. Even if there was no net income after the bills were paid in the ministry, the fact that people had jobs made the effort a worthy venture.

Unfortunately, many churches today are trapped in the annual "feel sorry for the poor people" syndrome, which complicates the problem. Free turkeys or clothing or Christmas gifts or annually volunteering at the shelter have become the accepted ways of helping for many Christians. What is needed is not pity, but opportunity. Offering jobs to the poor who can work will provide a sense of worth and dignity that no giveaway program could ever provide. Although relief ministries must exist to help those in need through crises or to help those who cannot work, development ministries that train, educate, and empower are desperately needed in our churches today. Church members must be taught to save or create small jobs to offer when someone asks for immediate financial help. One such experience may not immediately change a flawed system of assistance for that person; but if most Christians could learn to be generous through creating opportunities with dignity as a standard, the handful of manipulators will not spoil the system for those who do have dignity.

One of the best ministries a church can offer the poor is a job-training, job-finding, and job-coaching ministry. Asking church members to provide jobs as stewardship may be a new concept for some Christians, who would rather give a few dollars or clothes to an urban ministry; but few opportunities offer the long-term hope of overcoming poverty that this provides. Helping new employees adjust to the job with transportation assistance, occasional child care, budgeting assistance, and lots of encouragement may be necessary. Not all new workers are as easy as Russ, but most all can be groomed to become good employees who provide for their own families.

Ministry involvement at this level will likely demand a theological and practical mind change for many members. Though most will see the value in helping someone get a job, such efforts fall low in the evangelistic or missions priority list. Understanding that God cares for the whole person, not just the soul, may bring accusations of liberalism

one of the best ministries a church can offer the poor is a job-training, job-finding, and job-coaching ministry.

or misplaced priorities. Others may struggle with the cost, time, and slowness of such ministry. Development ministries require much more effort and take time to mature. Unlike mass efforts that touch a few folks lightly, these ministries involve ongoing relationships, discipleship, setbacks, disappointments, and perseverance. They demand encouragement for those who have been trapped in a system of cheapened charity seeking quick-fix approaches to patiently wait on the opportunities that God will provide as they remain faithful.

We will still need charity to fill the huge holes in the road to empowerment. We need assistance for orphans and widows and the severely mentally ill and physically disabled. We must still feed the hungry and give a drink of water to the thirsty. But in all of these loving responses, we must recapture the skill of helping the poor understand their own calling and regaining their own dignity.

RICARDO'S TRUTH
Be or find a family

The breakdown of the family in America makes God's family more crucial than ever. Churches must overcome our desire for comfort in order to fulfill our role as backup family for the many who desperately need it.

13

His mother pulled me aside after worship at Church Under the Bridge. "Ricardo ran away and is somewhere in Arizona, I think," she cried. "I don't know what to do." And indeed she did not have a clue. Ricardo had been the classic rebellious teen. At 14 he had done drugs and alcohol regularly, stolen a car, and run away. At 16, he was living with a girlfriend and being hunted by the police. His mother had done as much as she knew how to do. She tried to love him through the second painful divorce and child abuse from the stepdad. She had taken him to counseling at great expense to her meager job. She had certainly tried to raise him to understand the Lord and be active in church. None of it seemed to matter.

Through the years, his mother would keep me posted on which jail, prison, treatment center, or group home he was in. She only saw him a couple of times of year, but she never quit praying or lost hope that someday God would get ahold of him.

Somewhere along the line, Ricardo got tired of the rebellious and reprobate life he was living. Not unlike the prodigal son in the parable Jesus told, he virtually ended up in the pigpen of life. No money, no job, no one that really cared, his only resolve was to humbly return home and start over.

At 18, he found a little job, bought an old car, and began to move toward a responsible lifestyle. He would occasionally get discouraged and get drunk or drive too fast and get a ticket, but Ricardo's life had been changed and he was not going back to the emptiness of his adolescent past.

Now at 23 years of age, he sits on the front row with his fiancée and three children, the last one his. The mother and older girls came to faith and were baptized a year ago. Ricardo has a great job that demands some travel, but he never misses a Sunday. They know it's not right to live together as they do, and he and Melanie plan to be married in a few months.

As irony would have it, one of the young daughters recently climbed out of the bathroom window late one night and ran away. Suddenly awakened, Ricardo and Melanie realized within minutes what had happened and madly began searching for the 13-year-old. The police put out a search for her and within a few hours she was seen at a convenience store about 4:00 A.M. The police brought her home to his enormous relief, confusion, and anger at the stupidity of her act. Ricardo now understood what he had put his own mother through for years.

social angst

Raising a child in the midst of a growing pornographic culture of sin strikes fear in the hearts of every new father and mother who are aware of the culture. Drug and alcohol abuse, domestic violence, premarital sex, crime, and exploitation are all around us.

In our own community, one in five eighth-graders will use marijuana. Almost one in three (31 percent) children grow up below the federal poverty guideline. In Texas, one in four children will grow up poor and without health insurance. One in four adults is functionally illiterate. The state ranks 42nd of all states in spending on mental illness and mental retardation and near the bottom on education. Yet our prisons are full and considered one of the largest industries in the state. In our nation of "liberty . . . for all," 1 in 20 African American males will be imprisoned while in his 20s and only has a 1 in 76 percent chance of becoming a lawyer.

It is hard enough for resourced families who usually have strong support systems and a host of professional services behind them to raise a teenager through these difficult years. How much more is it to do so as a struggling single mom in the inner city?

The Loss of family

Well over half of the "trolls" who worship under the bridge have family dysfunction. Many, like Ricardo, left home years ago due to child abuse, sexual abuse, substance abuse, or hatred of some man living there with their mother. Most of the men never returned to their families of origin. Many of the women in the church ended up in several enmeshed relationships with men who abused them and their children. They eventually fled, only to have their poverty and loneliness lure them back into yet another messy relationship in another place and time. The church is filled with single, unattached men and women who have children that are struggling to make it.

The breakdown of the family in America is old news. For decades, the divorce rate, domestic violence, and sexual exploitation have unwoven God's tapestry of family, which was meant to be the place of safety, nurture, and growth. Instead, it became for many the seedbed of confusion, fear, and abuse, with emotional scars that go deep. Fractured families are the cause of much of today's poverty. Single mothers as heads of households with children stand clearly as the greatest single poverty group in America.

> single mothers as heads of households with children stand clearly as the greatest single poverty group in America.

In reaction to the work of James Dobson's Focus on the Family ministry, considered by some as a narrow, fundamentalist approach to the institution and definition of family, a bumper sticker was displayed on the backs of cars of those who disagreed with Dobson's values. The car message read, *Focus on your own #@!$ family.* Clearly, there are those who believe marriage, child rearing, and education are personal issues and hold to a view different from Dobson. Yet focusing on our families in the midst of ministry is important.

No one denies the importance of a healthy family. It is the place where meals are eaten together and the day's activities are discussed. It is a place where nurture and forgiveness and principles are communicated. It is clearly the best place to teach children about a loving God and His ways.

Urban ministry, broadly defined, is not just about working with under-resourced poor children living in housing projects. The city is the place where the best and the worst happen to families of all incomes, races, and worldviews. And any serious urban ministry must focus on the family.

A new family

In His mercy and grace, God seemed to always have a back-up plan for our lives. Although He created enough food for all to eat, He instituted systems that would guarantee opportunity for access to food for those who did not have it. He offered ways for orphans and widows to be cared for if fathers and husbands died unexpectedly. He even offered blood sacrifice for the sins of the people until His Son could offer His own blood for all humankind.

Knowing that our sin nature would frequently resist His best ways, God also provided a second family for those who would follow Him. The church is the family of God. The Bible clearly announces that followers of Christ become brothers and sisters and sons and daughters and mothers and fathers to each other. This extended family becomes the environment of inclusion, affirmation, discipline, teaching, and celebration. It is the place of rest, healing, and gentle shoves toward more responsibility.

But for those who have lost their family of origin, it is also the place of survival. The church is the family that rallies with the broken, broke, disheartened, unemployed, alone, and homeless. It becomes God's back-up plan for restoration for the poor and oppressed.

christian families should be different kinds of families

Christian families are the hope of the city. Churches are the extended families that widen the door for all. Yet to the average family and average church, these institutions are for personal safety, comfort, and privacy from the busy world of pain and multitasking. The last thing most families want is the intrusion or added dysfunction that someone in need would bring with them.

> christian families are the hope of the city.

So instead of inclusive families that have room for others in need, we have chosen to create institutions that are separate facilities with hired staff and clinical social workers. The homeless are put into shelters, the aged into nursing homes, and adolescents into juvenile detention centers. As good Christians, we support these institutions with our donations, but perhaps one of the core reasons that drives our giving is the hope that we do not have to get personally involved in the lives of those who are institutionalized.

"Let others do that because our family has enough to take care of at home," we say.

cell groups

Over the past 20 years, the church in the West has rediscovered the importance of the small group as a part of church life. More than Sunday School classes that teach good Bible lessons, these weekly small groups gather Christians around more intimate discipleship and accountability. Some are even outreach groups, which have found success inviting the unchurched, who refuse to go to religious sanctuaries, into their own homes. Relationships and vulnerability have become the keys to reclaiming the impersonal large-group worship. The cell group is the closest to the family context in most local churches. Because a person cannot have community with hundreds, these small home groups provide family-style nurturing.

But cell groups, like families, can turn inward and selfish. Our human nature wants to find places of comfort, which require little cross-cultural effort or emotional demand. Homogeneous groups flourish because they require the least amount of challenge.

Thus, if the church is seriously going to

offer its best ministry to the poor, hurting, and dysfunctional of society, the cell groups of the church are where urban ministry must primarily reside. Small Christian groups that will include those from other races, economic classes, and with social and emotional scars, can offer the greatest amount of love, discipleship, and healing. "For rich and poor to dine at the same table, eating the body and blood that unites them, is already a declaration of freedom from the world's standards, one which would by necessity change how these groups relate elsewhere in the community," says Lyle D. Vander Broek in *Breaking Barriers*. The group becomes the extended family, which gets involved in each other's lives, especially during hardship and challenging days. They offer encouragement, accountability, and opportunity while helping each other through the basic needs of food, clothing, and shelter. They celebrate birthdays, weep together in sadness, and play games together.

> The group becomes the extended family, which gets involved in each other's lives, especially during hardship and challenging days.

The problem is obvious. Such groups require significant time, energy, and some discomfort, the very things most folks have the least of to give. But if renewal in the urban centers ever occurs, it will not happen primarily through bigger and better nonprofit organizations, as much as they are needed as partners, but through churches that compassionately involve those individuals in our cities without personal familial relationships into their own families, both nuclear and congregational. Such bold restructuring would certainly receive opposition and create issues to work through together, but the early church understood this basic principle of Christian community (Acts 2:42–47; 4:36) and the result, "There were no needy persons among them." What a statement of Christians taking the gospel seriously!

CATFISH AND PILGRIM BILL'S TRUTH

The rich need the poor

God created the church as a body whose parts need each other to function properly. The rich need the poor to help them learn truths of the gospel from which they are blinded.

14

catfish was his street name, and nobody knew him by any other one. His name came from the long mustache he sported, which had extended whiskers like those on the mouth of a catfish. He lived in a homeless camp with several others at the edge of the railroad tracks. Everyone liked him. He was a committed Christian who knew his stuff and loved to dialogue, especially with college and seminary students.

On one occasion, I was asked to speak about the issue of homelessness at the local seminary, so I grabbed Catfish and two others to accompany me to my talk and add their thoughts. The first two homeless folks talked about their past struggles and current challenges, giving a personal side to the issue which most men and women in theological training had not heard. But when Catfish spoke, he was straightforward and prophetic. "You folks sit around talking about theology and religious stuff all day, but you seem to have ignored some of God's basic teachings about people like us," he said, looking at them in the eyes. "God cares for the poor and hurting people out on the streets of this community and we don't see you out there much." The students began to squirm a little. "You're just like all the Pharisees in Jesus's time, who acted high and mighty religious, but ignored the same people that Jesus came to connect with. What's the deal with that?" he queried. And then he said what surprised all of us, "I'm not sure you're even Christians!"

In the awkwardness of the moment, I tried to take the edge off his prophetic statement, but it remained tense. A student jumped back in with the question to Catfish, "Why don't you think we may not be Christians?" "Cuz you don't do what the Bible says toward the poor. Doesn't it say, 'Be doers of the Word and not hearers only'?" More dialogue ensued and points were clarified. As the class ended, a healthy tension remained about the relationship of word and deed. But most of the students came to understand that relationships with the poor were critical.

A two-way street

The basic assumption held by most middle-class Christians is that they are here to help the poor and unfortunate. Very few of them understand how much they need the poor in their own lives to help them grow in faith and understanding. Relationships between rich and poor change both parties. Just ask any wealthy person who has left the comfort of his or her own culture and gotten involved among struggling folks. Most will say something like this, "I went over to that part of town to help them, but what I discovered is how much they helped me!" And it is true. The poor, oppressed, sick, imprisoned, hungry, and mentally ill all teach us about the most important things in life, to which those with wealth often become blinded. They are God's best teachers.

The role of the resourced Christian is to proclaim the new identity of the poor who have joined the family of God as equals in the family. The poor are not projects, but persons made in the image of God and also called to be servants with us. "This identity empowers them to believe that God's purpose for them is that they be stewards and that all the power of God is available to them to overcome the forces of evil that prevent them from exercising and fulfilling stewardship," say Vinay Samuel and Chris Sugden in *Mission as Transformation*.

> The poor are not projects, but persons made in the image of God and also called to be servants with us.

XOX

sell all and follow me

The bearded man with the long walking stick just appeared under the bridge one Sunday. He was relatively quiet, but clearly a man of peace. Each Sunday he returned, so I asked him to have coffee. He agreed. Pilgrim Bill was the name he chose, but I could tell by his speech and demeanor that he had not been a street pilgrim all his life.

He said he would tell me his story if I would not share it with the church. It went like this. Bill was a licensed veterinarian who had worked hard and made lots of money. He had a wife and two children and a huge home in the Metroplex with not one, but two, swimming pools. He drove fancy cars, had all the latest electronic gadgets, and hung out on the golf course at the country club. But he was miserable. Life felt empty and lonely. There had to be more.

Through some unusual and providential situations, Bill chose to get involved in a Bible study with some Christians who meant business. He was fascinated by what he read and how seriously these new acquaintances struggled to understand and apply what they read. For months, he attended. He quit going to the social gatherings and golf course so he could spend more time learning from these followers of Jesus. He began to share his joy and interest with his family, but they were not interested. In fact, they were a little worried about the apparent changes.

Then one day Bill decided to become a Christ follower too. It was a huge decision and one celebrated by all his Bible study friends. So without knowing otherwise, Bill began to live out the same lessons he had read about in the Scriptures. He knew his prestige and possessions had entangled his life, so he left his high society life and then sold his new car. He started giving money to local Christian charities and visiting churches in search of a home. He refused to buy designer suits and clothing that had been his trademark. He began to hang out with his wife and children as much as possible. And he began to hang around the local homeless shelter, building new friendships with them.

His family was panicky and wanted him to get counseling. Something was wrong. It was OK to them if he got a little religion, but he was taking it too far. And when Bill announced he had decided to sell their mansion home to downsize, enough was enough. His wife gave him the ultimatum, either change back like he had been or get out.

So he got out. With sadness that his own wife could not let go of the world she had been enmeshed in and join his new joy-filled Christian life, he closed and sold his practice, gave the family the money, and hit the streets. He had been living as a homeless person for almost a year when we had coffee that day. He had found a small night job at one of the local kennels so he could make enough money to live on and enough to provide some assistance for others on the streets whom he befriended.

I have never met a man so deeply at peace in my life. Though he camped out in the cold, had been "rolled" a couple of times, and missed his family, there was a joy within his eyes like few seekers ever find. He was content and loved Jesus.

so what about me?

The immediate reaction from most Christians is that Jesus does not require such radical lifestyles of us to be Christian. Maybe, or maybe not. Certainly, the simple lifestyle alone does not make one a believer. But as most of us who explore the Scriptures seriously recognize, there is so much more to following Jesus than we are willing to do. Reducing faith to the minimum expectations is hardly faith at all. The dynamic power of the gospel continually calls us to repentance, change, and greater obedience. The complexities and stuff of our lives have become thorny vines around our good intentions, choking out the fruit of our faith. They steal from us the confidence of "being certain of what we do not see" (Hebrews 11:1) and putting our trust in God's provision instead of our own flesh.

The poor and marginalized of society have less to entangle them and more need to pray. Those who live one day at a time often have a prayer life and a faith that is more vital and real than those of us who are "neither hot nor cold." Those who are sick or in prison or addicted or homeless often have a humility that most of us middle-class Christians do not share in our arrogance and self-confidence. And many of the fellow strugglers of life know the importance of sharing and real generosity. They have discovered that the Lord of the streets was compassionate toward the poor and marginalized and "in the face" of the religious and wealthy. They found Jesus to be a friend who understands and cares.

We must each acknowledge the hardening processes that our sin and culture have on us. In the midst of this confession, we must allow God to refresh our first love and desire to find the pearl of great price at whatever cost. Truth cannot be compromised or found at a discount.

Reducing faith to the minimum expectations is hardly faith at all.

And what about the church?

The renewal of the church is critical as an agent of change in society. "For a radical gospel (the biblical kind) we need a radical church (the biblical kind). For the ever-new wine we must continually have new wineskins. In short, we need a cataclysm," says Howard A. Snyder in *Radical Renewal.* It will not come without a price. Change is hard and most church leaders and members are not willing to reevaluate and work through the difficult issues. It is easier to just be the same and wish things would get better. But Christians are compelled to challenge each other in the context of love to grow past their selfishness, greed, and exclusiveness. They must occasionally even openly critique each other as Paul did with Peter when he opposed him "to his face" (Galatians 2:11). According to David J. Bosch in *Transforming Mission,* "Believers cannot accept one another as members of a community of faith without this having consequences for their day-to-day life and for the world."

Mission, not missions, is the essence of

> Truth cannot be compromised or found at a discount.

and
Truth

the church. Sent by God, the church is the sign of the kingdom on the earth and cannot take this responsibility lightly. According to the book *Missional Church,* edited by Darrell L. Guder, "A missional ecclesiology challenges the church to be intentional about its unique social potential. Congregations should reflect the full social mix of the communities they serve, if they are truly contextual. Taking this approach will require substantial changes on the part of many congregations and most denominations."

It took Jesus making a whip of cords (John 2:15) and turning over the tables of the greedy sellers and moneychangers in His Father's house to get their attention. He yelled, "Get these out of here!" (John 2:16) to those who sold doves in the place of worship. The act was premeditated, not spontaneous or out of some fit of anger. God's house was a place of prayer, not commercialism. Let them arrest Him, but the truth could not be compromised.

The truth of the kingdom cannot be cheapened and be the gospel. We must somehow balance our children's Bible story images of God in the flesh, the prophets, and the apostles with their courageous stands against the institutionalism of religion that was tainted and compromised. We must question selling Jesus T-shirts and faddish WWJD bracelets in the place of worship, in the midst of a billion dollar religious product industry. We must occasionally stand up in business meetings and ask if our church budgets and programs are in keeping with the Gospels and priorities of our Lord. We must talk about the hard sayings of Jesus and get back to a biblical and theological foundation of the church, which remains "in" the culture but not "of" the culture. And we need to listen to those troll-like folks who are on the fringes of our society, and pray that someday they will tell us that what they see and hear from us is consistent with the life-changing message of Jesus. The trolls may just be right.

Bibliography

Alford, Deann. "A Bridge Over Troubled People," *Christianity Today*, April 2004, 71–75.

Bakke, Ray. *A Theology as Big as the City*. Downers Grove, IL: InterVarsity Press, 1997.

Bosch, David J. *Transforming Mission: Paradigm Shifts in Theology of Mission*. Maryknoll, NY: Orbis Books, 1991.

Bradshaw, Bruce. *Bridging the Gap: Evangelism, Development and Shalom*. Monrovia, CA: World Vision Resources, 1994.

———. *Change Across Cultures: A Narrative Approach to Social Transformation*. Grand Rapids, MI: Baker Academic, 2002.

Broek, Lyle D. Vander. *Breaking Barriers: The Possibilities of Christian Community in a Lonely World.* Grand Rapids, MI: Brazos Press, 2002.

Cheyne, John R. *Incarnational Agents: A Guide to Developmental Ministry.* Birmingham, AL: New Hope Publishers, 1996.

Christian, Jayakumar. *God of the Empty-Handed: Poverty, Power and the Kingdom of God.* Monrovia, CA: World Vision Resources, 1999.

Conn, Harvie M., ed. *Planting and Growing Urban Churches: From Dream to Reality.* Grand Rapids, MI: Baker Academic, 1997.

Conn, Harvie M., and others. *The Urban Face of Mission: Ministering the Gospel in a Diverse and Changing World.* Phillipsburg, NJ: P & R Publishing, 2002.

DeYoung, Curtiss Paul, and others. *United by Faith: The Multiracial Congregation as an Answer to the Problem of Race.* New York: Oxford University Press, 2003.

Dorrell, Jimmy. "I'm Loved Here." *Prism* Magazine, July/August 2005, 10, 11.

Emerson, Michael O., and Christian Smith. *Divided by Faith: Evangelical Religion and the Problem of Race in America.* New York: Oxford University Press, 2000.

Guder, Darrell L., ed. *Missional Church: A Vision for the Sending of the Church in North America.* Grand Rapids, MI: William B. Eerdmans Publishing Company, 1998.

Hughes, Philip E. *The Second Epistle to the Corinthians. New International Commentary on the New Testament.* Grand Rapids, MI: William B. Eerdmans Publishing Company, 1962.

Hardy, Lee. *The Fabric of This World: Inquiries into Calling, Career Choice, and the Design of Human Work.* Grand Rapids, MI: William B. Eerdmans Publishing Company, 1990.

Kunjufu, Jawanza. *Adam! Where Are You? Why Most Black Men Don't Go to Church.* Chicago, IL: African American Images, 1994.

Lupton, Robert D. *Renewing the City: Reflections on Community Development and Urban Renewal.* Downers Grove, IL: InterVarsity Press, 2005.

Moreau, A. Scott, and others, eds. *Deliver Us From Evil: An Uneasy Frontier in Christian Mission.* Monrovia, CA: World Vision Resources, 2002.

Ortiz, Manuel. *The Hispanic Challenge: Opportunities Confronting the Church.* Downers Grove, IL: InterVarsity Press, 1993.

Paul, Greg. *God in the Alley: Being and Seeing Jesus in a Broken World.* Colorado Springs, CO: Shaw Books, 2004.

Ronsvalle, John, and Sylvia Ronsvalle. "Giving to Religion." *Christian Century,* June 3–10, 1998, 579–81.

Sample, Tex. *Hard Living People and Mainstream Christians.* Nashville, TN: Abingdon Press, 1993.

Samuel, Vinay, and Chris Sugden. *Mission as Transformation: A Theology of the Whole Gospel.* Oxford, England: Regnum Books, 1999.

Sider, Ronald J. *Good News and Good Works: A Theology for the Whole Gospel.* Grand Rapids, MI: Baker Books, 1999.

————. *Just Generosity: A New Vision for Overcoming Poverty in America*. Grand Rapids, MI: Baker Books, 1999.

————. *Rich Christians in an Age of Hunger*. Nashville: W Publishing Group, 1997.

Smeeding, Timothy M., and Peter Gottschalk. "Cross-National Income Inequality." *Focus* 19, no. 3 (Summer/Fall 1998): 16–18.

Snyder, Howard. A. *Radical Renewal: The Problem of Wineskins Today*. Houston: Touch Publications, 1996.

Wolff, Edward. *Top Heavy: A Study of Increasing Inequality of Wealth in America*. New York: Twentieth Century Foundation, 1994.

Yancey, George. *One Body, One Spirit: Principles of Successful Multiracial Churches*. Downers Grove, IL: InterVarsity Press, 2003.

New Hope® Publishers is a division of WMU®, an international organization that challenges Christian believers to understand and be radically involved in God's mission. For more information about WMU, go to www.wmu.com. More information about New Hope books may be found at www.newhope publishers.com. New Hope books may be purchased at your local bookstore.

other Books
you may enjoy

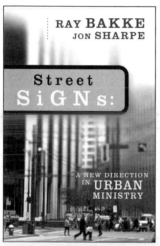

Street Signs
A New Direction in Urban Ministry
By Ray Bakke and Jon Sharpe
ISBN 1-59669-004-6

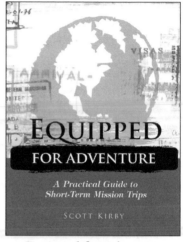

Equipped for Adventure
A Practical Guide to Short-Term Mission Trips
By Scott Kirby
ISBN 1-59669-011-9

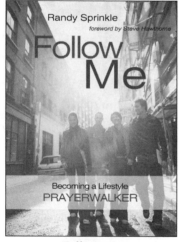

Follow Me
Becoming a Lifestyle Prayerwalker
By Randy Sprinkle
ISBN 1-56309-948-9

Available in bookstores
everywhere

For information about these books
or any New Hope products, visit
www.newhopepublishers.com.